"A vivid portrait of what happens to children thrust into combat."
~Blue Ink Review~

"Profoundly moving"
~Heather Osborne~

"Emotionally charged"
~Cheryl E. Rodriguez~

"A gripping story."
~Anne-Marie Reynolds~

"Hartness's harrowing and significant debut
succeeds. Comparisons to Ishmael Beah's *A Long
Way Gone: Memoirs of a Boy Soldier* are apt."
~Amy O'Loughlin- Forward Clarion Review~

AMANI'S RIVER

Amani's River

David Hartness

To order additional copies of this book, contact:
Xlibris
1-888-795-4274
www.Xlibris.com
Orders@Xlibris.com
700134

Contents

This book is dedicated to the 250,000 active child soldiers, whose courage and story gave the inspiration for this book. I pray for your safety and hope that you find the loving embrace that you deserve.

ACKNOWLEDGMENT

First and foremost, this book is dedicated to my mother, who believed in me when people said I could not pursue a life of academia solely based on a test. She fought back, said I can do anything if I work hard. I believed her, and I wrote my own success and followed my dreams with her cheering me on in the corner.

Many organizations have helped shape my life and provide purpose for my goals and ambitions. None more so than Waskowitz Outdoor School, who has helped me grow professionally and allowed me to believe that you can make a difference in the world through small acts of kindness. To all those who work for Waskowitz or volunteered, I thank you and acknowledge the support and love you have shown me. To the U.S. Peace Corps, thanks for sending me to Mozambique, challenging my way of thinking and providing support in my journey. Without the organization, this book would not be published.

I would like to thank my family for the constant support you have shown. Shilah's and James's constant encouragement of my professional dreams was tremendously helpful. Luke, you have been a constant supporter of my work and even sacrificed your own needs to encourage and support this project.

To Jequecene Comanhane, Elisa Lucas Chirrime, and your family, thanks for taking me in during my stay in Mozambique. Your love, support, and encouragement will not be forgotten.

To the rest of my family and friends, far too many to list, thanks for the stream of support.

PART 1

2013, Homoine, Mozambique

CHAPTER 1

I dare you to look into my eyes and get to know a deeper darker secret, which I have held since a child. A secret that makes it hard to see through the tough dexterity, which hides the pain but has traumatized my whole childhood. All that can be seen is the face of a broken man, with the duality of good and evil. The ambivalent emotions, which lie deep within, cannot be fixed. Few people have gotten the chance to crack open the hard shell and stare into the complex emotions, understanding the haunting dreams and forcing a life of fear because of the crimes committed.

They call me Aderito Chirindza, and I rest on the banks of the river near Homoine, Mozambique. I am in my early forties, skinny, and stand at less than six feet tall and have no unique characteristics, when completely clothed. If seen on the streets, you wouldn't be bothered to take a second glance; and if you were told I was a trained killer, you would think of this as lying, but the truth is spoken.

The sun streamed through the small cracks of the trees, and the wind blew in circles. The water plunged downstream, as I was content with a mesmerizing stare at the ripples swaying and twirling in a desynchronized pattern, with a distinct rhythm. The sweet smell of the low-rushing river and the green and natural surroundings brought a peaceful memory back, one of the last of this place. I took in deep breaths and closed my eyes, remembering the feeling of peace, sitting in this very spot as a child.

My eyes opened and glanced at the gold urn, which rubbed close to my side. Peaceful memories escaped my reflection, and deep sadness came crashing into ever-changing and complex thoughts.

Mozambique brought destruction into my life. Images of death, blood, and tears flashed in my mind; and as much as it needed to stop, the incessant running slideshow couldn't be terminated.

My posture sagged, knees pressed against my chest, and arms dangled toward the ground between my legs. The depression I spent so many years trying to escape came flooding back with the sheer presence of the country I absconded from so many years ago. My chest felt hollow as pain entered and my pulse crawled.

I fixated on the far-end slope where there was an infant Chlorocebus monkey swinging and jumping around on a nearby branch. My eyes squinted from a small glimmer of light, which illuminated my face. The small light did not force me to walk or cower behind the shade of the tall trees that lined the riverbanks. The innocence of the infant playing in his own world, careless and free from the dangers that may lurk in the dense wooded area, preoccupied the changing mood. It swung from branch to branch, disturbing the woods and forcing small insects to scatter around as their home was destroyed. A small smile broke free as the little baby ate an insect that passed by. The infectious, playful manner made me wish that my childhood had been this free.

The mother entered from behind a tree and grabbed the baby, placing him under the abdomen where he grabbed tightly to the thick fur. She stopped and stared into my eyes, and as if she sensed the pain and horror of my life, she became frightened and agitated. She didn't understand what the pain was but saw it in me. Quick to find an abrupt exit, the monkey turned and rushed back into the thick woods, and soon all that was heard was the crunching of sticks and branches of trees swaying vigorously.

My son's voice off in the distance brought my thoughts back. The loud laughter of the teenager watching another monkey move throughout, eating a banana, allowed the grief to escape. Michael appeared simple, chasing the monkey into the woods, without the intent of malicious behavior. His smile stretched across his face, forcing his thin cheeks to wrinkle toward his eyes, and the bright smile and loud laughter echoed in the valley. His smile was bright and colorful, and body movements bounced, happy in his own world.

Michael had on a pair of tan-colored shorts that stretched below his knees and a striped polo T-shirt. Michael was smaller than I was but had broad strong shoulders from playing sports at his local school. You wouldn't have noticed this because his clothes were two sizes too big, which covered up the forming muscles.

The deep stare of my glazing eyes into the jovial child allowed past image of my youth, ripped away from atrocities of being a child soldier in a war, in which I wasn't mature enough to understand, escape. Images of when I was sixteen, sitting in therapy, desperate to find my smile and joy in life that Michael felt, unaware of my violent history. This thought brought the slideshow of the struggles back. I wished it would abandon my dreams, but the memories lingered.

"Michael . . . come here," I shouted.

Michael jogged over and sat a few inches from my torso. I looked back out at the river and listened to the sounds of the birds chirping and the river eloquently rushing over the rocks and splashing on the banks. Women could be heard washing clothes while children played and splashed in the water. The wind subtly carried their voices, but I could not see them. Michael was looking toward me, waiting for a response or waiting for a reason for him being called, but none would be given to the perplexed boy.

"Listen to that river, Michael," I said in a soft, gentle voice, swaying in the same rushing, pounding rhythm, with my eyes closed tight. "Sounds beautiful!"

"I guess," Michael stated, unaware of the simple pleasures, which took over two decades to find.

Michael's eyes darted away and became glued to a stick placed within arm's reach. Michael grabbed the switch and started to push the bare patch of dirt, which was surrounded by the green grass that was freshly cut from the goats grazing the land in the morning. He continued to spread dirt out toward the grass, making the patch larger, as he waited for the moment to speak and suffice his curiosity. "Why are we here?" Michael finally stated.

"I spent some of my childhood playing in this river."

Michael's eyes widened, and his head shot up to glare into my eyes, as he dropped the stick and suddenly found an interest. "You lived in Africa?"

"Yes!"

"Why did you leave?"

"It . . . it was time," I said, raising my eyebrows and stuttering to an answer.

"So why did we bring Grandma's ashes to this place?"

As Michael said Grandma, his eyes went back to the ground, and his face became grim as if he had forgotten his grandma had died. The simple mention of the name brought emotions back, which Michael didn't understand.

Jennifer, an alluring woman, walked up behind, returning from her stroll down the riverbank. She had long silky black hair, with a waist that curved like the sparkling river. Jennifer had soft lips and an innocence that looked as if she had not experienced any pain. Her eyes were kind and gave off the courage and attraction of a woman you wanted to accompany. These qualities were the reason I married her.

She sat next to us and rested her head on my shoulder. She clasped her hand with mine and smiled gently. Our eyes met; and then I gave her a small grin, kissing her soft lips, which lasted a few seconds. But the slight sensation of the lipstick lingered in my mouth longer.

"Are you going to finally tell us why it was so important to spread your mom's ashes at this river?"

I gave a deep breath, and a small tear rolled the length of my cheek, landing on my blue jeans. Silence persisted as I listened once more to the soft, subtle sound of the river. I took one more subdued warm breath, and then . . . began my story . . .

PART 2

1982, Traveling

CHAPTER 2

This story starts in a small house in Houston, Texas. I was ten years old at the time and smaller than the rest of the children, but this was to be expected because my father stood five feet four inches, and Mother wasn't much taller. I was a scrawny little kid, which made me an easy target for the bullies; and as a result, I wasn't skilled at sports and always had a hard time making friends. For the most part, I liked being an outsider, sitting on the playground at the local elementary school, watching people pass by, paying no attention to the kid that provided no immediate masculine threat to their superiority.

Two other people at my school cared less about the societal pressures of being "the cool kid" who could do anything and be anything, and so out of a process of elimination, we became friends. Many lunches were hence spent sitting immersed in silence, watching the various children pass by, unaware that three nobodies sat present. The awkward stare into silence, immersed in a process of thought, which would appear jumbled and confusing to most but seemed so relevant and important at the time. There was no immediate need to make conversation because most of what needed to be said wasn't important.

Many days in class were spent staring out the lancet, pretending to be the brave adventurer, planning and plotting his escape. The teacher stood in front of the class, but I gave her little of my attention until my name was shouted several times for an answer. Back into reality, I could only stutter a few words of nonsense, allowing the class to erupt with laughter. My time as a child was spent confused; but I would hardly call myself a retard, nerd, or loner, which were words often shouted at me from a distance, followed by giggles, and then silence. I would call myself a child content with living in my own mind. It wasn't that conversations with others scared me, or I wasn't skilled at conversing with living humans; simply put, I enjoyed my own conversations more.

The school bell rang, and I slowly walked out of the wide metal-framed doors, as children rushed and pushed their way past. This didn't force my speed to increase. Steadily, I walked out with my head hanging low, kicking a small pebble that was found at the exit of the school. The daily routine commenced, where I slowly walked down the street to my small home in the suburbs of Houston. As I entered the house, my dad sat in a darkened kitchen with his hands clasped tight together and his knuckles resting on his chin. His eyes looked toward the plastic-lined table with a yellow-and-blue flower print around the edges and a solid white top. My dad was never home when I arrived; in fact, I usually arrived to a locked door and an empty house. The perplexity of his appearance and sadness in his face forced my eyes to widen and my brows to rise to my forehead.

My dad, Amani Chirindza, grew up in Mozambique but never spoke of has past life. I know he immigrated to the United States during the time when the Portuguese ruled, but many of the family stayed behind during the independence and the civil war. The brutal ruling party of Mozambique that reigned over the blacks with an iron fist drove my father to dream of far-off places and ultimately to struggle for his relief of the strong arms of the Portuguese army. The Portuguese had been in power since they colonized the country in 1505. They drove the blacks to slavery, beat them into submission, and treated them like second-class citizens with no rights or freedoms to express their views in their own country. The segregation of the 1960s and into the 1970s, when my father was a young man unable to scale the large white fences and take diplomatic stands against the whites, tugged at my father's ambitions. Realizing the struggle was too large, he fled the country before the start of the civil war in hopes of the American dream.

The civil war started in 1977, just two years after the fight for independence. The war started as a diplomatic struggle where the Mozambique Resistance Movement (RENAMO), receiving funding from Rhodesia, was opposed by the party that would later seize power, the Front for the Liberation of Mozambique (FRELIMO). The opposition of these struggles led the country into deep division, forcing the citizens to fight brothers and sisters for hopes of a democratic society. RENAMO took their fight and terrorized small towns and rural areas while FRELIMO controlled the larger cities, forcing them to fight against hundreds of far-reaching and dense areas. The strategies led to a sixteen-year war, where five million innocent people were affected, blood shed, lives lost, and land and large villages burned. The lush vegetation turned to ashes and smoke while the animals fled to safer lands, leaving the large country free from the beautiful nature Africa is known to have. The brutal war was worn on the faces and actions of men, women, and children, some too naive to understand the struggle they were born into.

The clothes my father wore were as mundane as his personality. His bland polo shirts and ironed slacks identified his style, as he never liked to underdress for any occasion. The small visible mustache stood as a symbol of the stern persona that many associated with my father. It was rare that Dad smiled or made jokes of any nature. The introverted tendency that defined him was where I acquired the wish to spend time with my thoughts and examine the world from a singular perspective. The enjoyment of peace and never speaking unless it proved to be important and meaningful to the conversation was a characteristic that became a part of our life. On the rare occasion that we presided at a party, we lingered in the same spot, and it was rare that we sought out the adventures of a conversation.

My mother and father met in 1971 and that same year brought me into this world. They married after my birth; and now, ten years later, we lived in a small home in the center of town.

Michelle Chirindza, a woman who had a contagious smile, which infected people in the most profound ways, appeared more pleasant than my father. Mom wasn't afraid to get dirty or wear clothes that may be less than appealing to the eyes. But when she did dress for a party, everyone looked upon reflection on her eloquence. Dad and I hid behind her powerful words and would follow her lead in any social situation.

Finally, I found a resting place in my own world, on the brown carpet, leaning against the seventies plaid couch, where I watched the blank TV with rabbit ears stretched toward the ceiling. The TV was tan with a silver turn dial to change to the five different channels that came through the old tube, which sat centered on a flimsy black TV stand.

I grabbed a book that lay on the old couch and soon immersed myself in the adventures of Omri in *The Indian and the Cupboard*. I preferred the quiet nature of reading as supposed to the ruckus and mindless noise from the TV. Many children may find that strange, but I felt it was normal.

My mother soon joined my father, and the two sat in the kitchen and conversed in a significant manner due to their conspicuous demeanor and low whisper. This clue indicated they were in the middle of a conversation that wasn't meant for young ears. This was an often occurrence, so it did not pique my curiosity, and the conversations wielded nothing of importance. Therefore, I continued to read, trying to tune them out and focus on Omri and the toy Indians that came to life.

Forgetting the secret conversation in the kitchen, I rose from the floor and headed into the other room for a drink. The conversation halted as they looked at me grabbing a cup from the bottom cupboard and turning on the faucet to fill the glass with lukewarm water. Oblivious to the fact they had stopped and stared at my activities, I continued turning around to be met by four eyes staring at my clueless physique. I stopped briefly to think about the awkward eyes that gazed upon and pondered the exit strategy.

As the next move floated in my mind, my mom was gracious enough to alleviate the tension by stating, "Tell him Amani," she demanded. "Amani Chirindza . . . tell him." Mom never used his last name, so I guessed that there was a pressing issue.

"I will tell him after dinner . . . I need time to think," my father shouted and removed himself from the table in a hurry.

My father always carried a stern nature, and many people were nervous to approach him. He carried his back straight and shoulders stretched wide. He never said much, but when he did, he carried a firm and demanding presence. I saw him to be gentle and generous, where others saw brute and isolation.

My mother was different from my father as she was proper in the way she walked and the warm and welcoming tone in her voice that brought comfort to many. However, being demanding was never easy, and she often lost arguments because of the desire to please others.

The brief conversation had sparked my curiosity. Up until this point, their secrecy had captivated little interest; but now this was what passed through my thoughts. By the sound of the soft whisper, I guessed that the conversations had something to do with me and that it wasn't something adults could commend.

I had never seen my mother that upset. Dad had made this decision on his own. My father was a delightful yet hard-to-read man, but when he reached a decision, there was nothing that could be said to change his mind. The stubborn characteristic had led to several misguided decisions, but none paralleled this.

The rest of the morning and into the afternoon, I sat reading and occasionally played with toys. Even though, by outside appearances, I showed satisfaction with these distractions, my thoughts pondered everywhere but on the youthful play. I thought maybe divorce was in the future or my dad got a new job, which found us living in a new state. As hard as I tried, the purpose of the conversation was less comprehensible, and the only thing that was a certainty was that this affected me and most likely left feelings of dejection.

Dinner soon came, and we took the seats at the regular places. My father sat at the head of the table, while Mother and I sat on either side. The three of us had our eyes on the plate in front and didn't dare take a glance at each other, knowing that to be the grim signal to have a serious colloquy. I wanted to find out, but my stomach turned in knots as my nervous ten-year-old body dreaded the news. My parents didn't speak, and the only sound that came from the table was the clanging of silverware and the crunching of food.

The last bit of juicy tender steak went into my mouth, and now the moment when the big escape happened, and I could rush away. My gentle hands placed the fork soft on the white plate, covered with tomato sauce, trying to make as little noise as possible. My mother and father had their heads lowered and eyes in a deep stare with their disappearing dinner, so I pushed the chair back and lifted myself from the table. I walked away on the tips of my toes. As I crept past, a strong relief filled my heart. I had escaped the dreaded news and walked faster, approaching the door, at the end of the corridor, in front of the dinner table. My father's dark stern voice rang through the house and echoed off the walls.

"Aderito . . . come here."

The voice sounded as if I had done something wrong. My mind jumped around the last few days, trying to think of what actions or inaction I did that was so wrong to make my parents agitated. The possible rebellious action forced my tiny mind to go back and forth, trying to come up with an excuse, but alas, the efforts were pointless as the cause of the yelling was unknown.

I walked back to the table, with my head lowered and hands gripped behind my back, palms saturated in sweat, and stomach turned into knots. My body rocked as I took my place back at the table and caught a glimpse of my mother, whose face filled with deep sadness, but her body stood up straight as she tried to be strong, but strong sadness resonated on her scared face.

My father's eyes lowered toward his empty plate as he was trying to collect his thoughts and trying to find the perfect words to express the decision he had made. The strong and righteous man thought that he always made the best decisions. Fear was never a part of him as he was a protector and made sure that every decision was the best for the family. My eyes moved back over at my mother where I sensed the disagreement and knew that she felt powerless to his presence and his influence within the family.

"Michael," he said, pausing before he continued, "are you aware that I come from Mozambique?"

I gave him a slight nod.

"Five days ago, I received a call from your uncle who is still in Mozambique. He said the country is not doing well, and so I talked to the priest . . . at our church and asked if I can go on a mission . . . back to Mozambique. I have made the decision that we will leave in three weeks and stay until I can guarantee that my family is safe and free."

An eerie silence lingered as I pondered the news and what it meant. I didn't know what to think. I didn't know my uncle or any of my family in Mozambique. Everything that I enjoyed was in Houston—friends, family, and school—resided here; and I knew nothing of the outside world.

"What? I can't move. What about school . . . friends?" I said, shocked, with my eyes wide open and face lowered, trying to sell the disbelief to my father. "What about the violence? Have you and Mom talked about the civil war? What will happen to me . . . to Mom if we get caught up in the violence?"

The term echoed in the silent house as I paused for dramatic effect and sensed that the momentum of the argument was in my favor, and I couldn't be stopped as I pleaded multiple points.

"What if we die? What will you do then?" My voice rose as the argument continued.

The search for an answer was cut short as my father yelled, "STOP!"

I never saw him yell at me, but when this happened, I stopped and shriveled backward. I jittered to a standstill and lowered my head as my argument proved pointless. I looked at my mother for advice and support but received nothing but a veiled attempt at holding her tears from being visible. A trickle of water rolled downward toward my cheek, then a second, and a third. I wiped the tears from my eyes and gazed at my father.

"Enough of this. The decision is made. In three weeks, we will leave for Mozambique. I don't want to see any more tears or hear any more arguments." My father paused and looked into my eyes. He slapped the table with his open hand. The plate that sat a few inches from him jumped. "Did you hear me? Will I hear any more of this nonsense? Wipe away those tears," he raised his voice.

"Yes, Dad." I wiped the tears away and stood up tall. I tried to keep my emotions in check. At least while in his presence.

"Good. Go to your room."

I walked past my father but didn't dare look into his eyes. Once past him, I ran to my bedroom, flung the door open, and then closed it with a soft touch, trying not to cause anxiety or anger. I jumped on my bed and buried my head into the pillow. Tears started to leave my eyes and saturate the sheets, and once they began, I couldn't stop.

I lowered my head deeper into the pillow and screamed, trying to mute the sounds of despondency. The bed was the brute of my anger as I kicked hard, trying in whatever means to get my anger out. Agitated, I lay, with tears still coming faster and faster and my chest rising and falling as if hyperventilating. My nose ran water as I sniffled and wiped them clean. Gasps of air came in and out. I grabbed the ends of the pillow and pulled hard, trying to rip them to shreds, but the gaunt arms could do little harm.

The only images I had of Africa were pictures I saw at school. Pictures of men who bared their chests, carrying spears and herding goats, and people who lived in the middle of the desert, away from civilization. Was this going to be my new life?

Why couldn't he go by himself? Why couldn't Mom and I stay here where it is safe? Questions arrived and passed without an answer, as it was futile. In three weeks' time, we would board a plane, heading to Mozambique.

I became weary and fell asleep, with my clothes buttoned and zipped to my body and my head resting on my hard damp pillow.

***

The next day I woke up, hoping that the news was a frightful dream; but upon the door swinging open, I walked out and saw my mother arranging boxes and father talking on the phone with a moving company.

In the bathroom, I turned on the hot water. Glancing into the mirror, I saw a face glaring back, with lines streaking through from the night's sleep. Disrobing, I stepped into the bath water and looked up at the ceiling, sitting and pondering the news. Toys sat a few feet away, but I didn't touch them. Bubble bath soap was sitting next to me, and I didn't use it, because what felt so pertinent a few days ago appeared less relevant today. Was this rage, depression, or, because my thoughts wandered, trying to understand my fate?

I sat in the warm water until it soon became cold but continued to sit there until the water was freezing, body shriveling, and I could bear it no more. I didn't want to leave because the second I did, I would have to face the days that lie ahead. This happened to be the days of the dreaded, mundane, pointless activities that led me one step closer to the rest of life.

CHAPTER 3

The last week in the United States moved insensibly through the mundane daily tasks of going to school, packing, and trying to keep from showing any hint of emotion. My two friends said nothing, but I sensed that they knew a secret was being hidden from them. This probably showed in my behavior as of late. There was a willingness to engage in mindless chatter, feeling the days and hours were numbered; and soon they would be a distant memory, fading from existence. The thought of telling them churned in my stomach, and I wanted to blurt it out; but the words couldn't be found, and so my muted mouth kept quiet. Therefore, the awkward endless conversations that yielded no purpose persisted. It wasn't that I wanted to keep the news a secret; it was the fact that I was leaving to a country that is known through the news agencies as a society under brutal violence. What would they think? Would they think my father was crazy? Or perhaps that I would die? I felt the same way. I wanted to leave the United States without anyone knowing, but the school found out because of my mom. She said we wanted to go on a church mission, working in a small hospital helping those affected by war.

The last day of school arrived. I entered the school grounds, scared, knowing the end was near. Knowing that it would be the last time I entered and soon the last time I exited. The end scared me because the beginning was so foreign. The future was a bleak, blurry mess that showed no real promise.

As I entered the long corridor toward my class, I saw children pass. Some who I didn't know, others who bullied me, and a few who were nice. I wanted to scream, drop to my knees, and cry. What a lasting image that would be to the rest of the kids, watching a scrawny young child flailing around like a fish but crying like a baby. Ultimately, I held my chin high, shoulders squared, and walked into the class.

The teacher told the rest of the class that I would soon leave. This came as a shock to the few friends I had, who now wondered why I had kept secrets from them. Of course, I didn't have an answer, so I shrugged my shoulders and left them forever. Saying good-bye to them was hard. But the saddest part was my dilemma.

During my last week, more research on Africa and on Mozambique was conducted, and I didn't find the information appealing. Images of life in a deserted place without people around me that spoke English continued to haunt me. Images with no shops and forcing to go to bed to the sounds of gunfire constantly ran through my mind. The thought of this as a common soothing sound heard for miles and might be needed for me to fall asleep, like the soothing sounds of raindrops, of normal children living a normal life. As my mind kept vacillating, I became more agitated, and my energy started to try to figure out ways that I could stop this from happening.

I talked with my mom in private, and I spoke with my grandparents to try to find a different place to live. However, every idea led to a dead end, which led to greater depression; and at the end of the week, I flew to Mozambique.

***

Once we arrived in Maputo, the capital city, no one appeared to greet our family. As we departed the plane, an intense stream of dry heat warmed our bodies, and the layers of clothes that we brought from the States appeared to be futile. The second we stepped on to the small tarmac of the tiny international airport, the ground appeared to wave back and forth, the sun beat on my face, and my throat shriveled. Energy escaped my body as I became tired. I took off my winter coat and then my blue long-sleeved shirt and soon strolled toward the small building in a tight-fitting white undershirt, exposing blots of sweat.

We waited for twenty minutes in the security checkpoint. The dreadful heat appeared to enter the building. In fact, it grew hotter inside, which forced the sweat to run in rivulets on my back. Once we reached the front of the line, we must have looked as if we stepped out of a sauna. Sweat seeped through my father's suit, and a large stain formed under his armpits. Mom's hair stuck to her face, and small stains formed on the back of her loose-fitting flower-printed dress.

Behind a large desk, a police officer sat, who checked passports. Dad did the speaking because he understood the language. The officer was more concerned with how much money we had to bribe him and less troubled with why we wanted to enter his country.

Once we had departed the airport and entered Mozambique, we hailed a taxi. The driver took us to a large dirt field where buses and vans parked one after another, which appeared to be an endless stretch of old torn vehicles. The buses were at least ten years old but abused and not looked after and carried the aura of thirty-year-old vehicles. Not one bus was new, and most had paint chipping off or a bumper dented and not fixed after a small accident. Each bus, once painted a fresh white, now looked browner from the thick dirt, with a dirty blue top.

A large bus passed. The engine sounded as if it were going to take its last breath until it puttered to a dead stop. Black smoke shot out from the exhaust pipe, and every time the wheel turned, it made a loud creaking sound.

Many people moved around, strolling in no particular direction, but more moved with a purpose in mind. People pushed through lines and shoved each other out of the way to get through the mob that formed and grew larger. This appeared to be a natural state of survival as no one was bothered with the abruptness of the people and moved, unfazed. I stayed near my mom, scared of the strange people that advanced through the crowd in no particular order, with no plan. What appeared to be a foreign and strange custom looked as if it were a daily chore where they didn't know any difference.

A man sat on the dirt ground a few feet away from a puddle of muddy water, created by many young boys washing a small van, trying to make extra money. His jeans tore at the knees and bottoms. The man had blotches of hair on his face, which made for a rough beard. His toenails looked yellow and unkempt, and his hands and feet hadn't been washed in several days. The long tangled hair made him look shabby and further pointed to proof that the man was homeless. Head to toe was painted with dirt and soot from the smoldering burned trash off in the distance. The man was in his forties but appeared to have aged through stress and trapped in a body of a much older man.

I glared at the man for a few minutes and wondered what he had done, the life he lived, and the crimes he committed to deserve a life of solitude. He looked up at me, and for a brief second, he stared into my eyes. I turned away, not wanting to appear to be gazing at anyone, unsure of how he might react.

As we walked through the dusty field, a bus appeared with a handwritten notice, on a cardboard box, that said Maxixe taped to the window. We stepped into the bus and took a seat in the front. The old bus had torn seats, many of which lost the foam that once made them comfortable. The bus smelled like trash and filled with people sweating from the forehead, trying to wipe themselves clean with small rags but unable to keep up with dripping sweat.

It was eighty degrees outside, and the bus felt a hundred inside. The heat forced me to sit next to the window where I looked outside at the people leaping over small puddles, brushing up against each other but moving in unison. Women carried woven baskets on their heads, balancing them without the support of their arms, as the arms were preoccupied with the infants. Men carried heavy loads of different marketable products with handmade wheelbarrows. The wheelbarrow looked different from the one we used to own in Houston. There was a handle with one small wheel. A long handmade compartment that stretched three feet past the main body of the wheelbarrow, which created an extensive steel shelf. This shelf could carry crates of beer, stacked on top of each other, which allowed the employee to collect more items in each load.

The bus filled up, but the driver refused to leave until people packed in the bus, so we stayed in the parking lot for an hour. More people entered, and once the seats were filled, I thought we were ready to leave; but the driver waited until people filled up the middle aisle. Once the bus was packed with people standing in the aisle and sitting on each other, it started up, and we left the muddy parking lot.

As the bus pulled through Maputo, I saw a few children playing in dirty water. The children, exposed, were running free in front of the passing people. The children couldn't care less of the people watching and the buses pulling out of the city. I couldn't help but smile and wonder why these children, around my age, could be comfortable enough to run around naked in public.

The thought of walking out of my house in my underwear sent shivers up my arm.

The water, which came from the sewer pipes, was mixed with oil that floated on top. Children, however, didn't seem to be bothered by the dark black water, mixed with a light-green lime that coated the outside pipe. They appeared unaware of the imminent hygiene issues or dangers and diseases that may be in the water, which was discussed in far too much detail in the States. Children gave off bright smiles, screamed, and yelled as they jumped in the water, as if it were the public pool. They hopped back out, pushed one another, and laughed louder. Adults passed by and said nothing. Others just smiled but allowed them their freedom to be children—careless and happy.

We continued to follow the turnaround. In the same water, a young child, a few years younger than me, squatted, with his pants to his ankles, dumping feces in the water. The strange and disgusting behavior appeared odd and out of place, and I couldn't grasp the child's actions. An innocent boy going to the bathroom, for people to see, and just a few feet downstream were children playing and bathing in the same filthy water. Did this boy not realize that the filth from his body was washing off to where his friends sat and played?

The driver turned off the turnaround and headed straight to the main road, which led us to Maxixe. Just before leaving Maputo, I saw two green trucks parked on either side of the two-lane highway. Standing in the back were several young men that held guns outward. The officers wore military-issued hard helmets that strapped under their chins and had long-sleeved green-and-tan-colored military shirts and pants that matched. Two military officers stopped traffic, with their guns strapped to their backs. They had various metals and ribbons pinned to their pressed uniform, indicating officers of importance. Tassels dangled from their solid shoulder pads, and they stood tall as our bus inched closer.

The leader talked to the driver in a language that was not comprehensible. Grabbing the license, he started to walk around the bus. My eyes followed him as he peered through each window and looked at each passenger. He glanced at the license and then back at the innocent people, trying to keep their eyes in front and not look at the officers. The officer passed me and slowly glanced into my eyes. Not willing to show his kindness, he kept his stern face, with the brim of his hat lowered close to his eyes, casting a small shadow over his face.

He soon handed the documents back to the driver and signaled for him continue on his journey.

Different officers stopped our bus multiple times, and each time, my stomach sank. I never knew what the mission was and if they were planning to turn the guns on the vehicles. I wished that someone spoke English who could explain this to me, but there was no one. My father tried to assure me that this was normal and that it was okay, but I didn't believe him. There were too many unknowns with these circumstances, which made me uncomfortable.

The whole ride, my eyes obsessed on the landscape and the passing people. Every inch of land, every person I saw, and every flame of fire that scattered the scenery became a fresh representation of my new life. When given a moment to think, I became scared but eager to see my new home and the village people that we needed to help. Throughout the ride, I looked to my mother for durability and comfort. She was willing to put on a strong manner and keep this for my sake.

***

Maxixe was a beach village and, therefore, sandy and further developed than many of the other small towns that we passed. A few hotels needed desperate attention. Many people roamed and sold things in the various colorful markets that lined the long stretch of streets. The village felt historical, with large Portuguese-made houses and office buildings with walled carvings and ceramic rooftop structures. These houses had been vacant from the Portuguese for a while and, because of this, sat untouched and not maintained. The pools were a strong indicator, which were drained of water, formed cracks around the wall, or filled with green water, becoming a breeding ground for mosquitoes.

The houses did not show any form of fresh paint, and the bushes that once produced vivid allure now provided a symbol of the dying economy. Casements and doorframes of the structural marvels now stood broken and torn apart. Glass broke, trash filled the lawns, and goats and chickens roamed free, adding their droppings to a place that by outside appearances looked desolate.

While in Maxixe, we met my uncle. The plan was to stay one night at their small home on the outskirts of the village and then the next day head to my new home, fifteen miles inland.

My uncle looked to be the twin of my father but more personable and heavier around the waist, which complemented his jovial smile. The clean-shaven and balding man, with bright eyes and crystal white teeth, never erased the smile. The smile he wore made him appear to be an affable man who was ecstatic to see his brother and receive my mom and me for the first time.

He led us away from the bus stop, where we entered the main stretch of road. Dark gray smoke rose to the skies off in the distance. As we approached the high-rising smoke, the smell intensified. Several tires, placed on the streets, with trash intermixed, burned a long black stream of smoke, causing a stark reminder of the poverty that surrounded my family. A child ran around the flames, screaming, with his arms stretched out and waving a stick. The child ran barefoot, through the paved road and small pebbles thrown on the street. A large smile broke free as he pranced around the fire. Other children joined. One pushed around a tubeless bike wheel while another joined in the wasted running.

We veered away from the fire and walked through many long alleyways. The walkway was large enough for a few people and maybe a bicycle. The uneven ground proved to be difficult to navigate. On either side of us, one home after another, lined the long alleyway. Many homes sat wide open, and we could see inside every room while other homes hid behind the protected makeshift fences made of different materials.

The women and children who occupied the compound appeared to be working, cooking, playing, or conversing with neighbors. Black smoke rose to the sky as people burned yesterday's trash of paper and plastic, which sent the smell of black smoke through my nose and throat, causing a subtle burning sensation.

As we walked, a gang of children came running by and brushed my shoulders, knocking me back. Up ahead, more unsupervised children played soccer in the narrow road but looked content with making their own amusement. The ball rolled through the bumpy walkway from one player to the next. Loud laughter erupted as one player missed the ball, which sent him running after to retrieve the prized possession that had problems holding air.

We arrived at my uncle's small two-bedroom home. Sitting in the compound ready to greet us were his wife, five children, and three cousins who lived in the home together. The concrete house had large pieces of cement chipped off the corners. At one time, the house had bright-yellow paint but now sat dim from the glaring sun. The roof was no different from the rest of the homes, as it was single sheets of tin roofing, angled to allow water to drain.

Walking inside the small home, I looked up at the ceiling, where I could see the rusted tin sheets, with small but visible holes, allowing slight beams of light to shine bright.

The house had no storage, and so possessions crammed in every corner and stacked onto each other. Pots, pans, plates, and dishes rested on the floor, crammed against the far wall. Next to these items sat a large dinner table that took most of the space.

There was one three-seat sofa and a single chair, which was hard and uncomfortable. I could see why the children enjoyed playing outside because their homes had no room for people to sit, chat, or play.

My aunt and uncle shared one room while the children slept in the other. The children's room had two mattresses spread out on the floor and placed in the corner were suitcases filled with clothes stacked on top of each other. There was no room to roam, and it was hard to imagine how the children found enough room to sleep together.

We talked with the family for a while, but everyone went to bed early. By 8:00 p.m., just after dinner, the children were ready to go to bed because they had to get up early to complete the morning chores of washing dishes and clothes and cleaning the house.

My uncle told me that I would sleep in the bedroom with the children. Nine people filtered into the small room. The children took their clothes off and stood in the middle of the room in their underwear. They weren't bashful to expose themselves in this manner. The children's ages ranged from six to seventeen, with each developing at different stages, yet the idea of private areas and indecent exposure had little concern within the culture. They didn't have any clothes to sleep in, so this was the best that they could do. There was a long pause as they waited and looked toward me, curious as to why I did not strip and prepare for bed. Once established that I would sleep in my clothes, the lights turned off, and the rest of the children fell asleep.

I didn't know these people, and I wasn't going to spend the night sleeping with other children in my underwear. I lay next to nine children: four girls and five boys. I was on the far end, closest to the door. It was hard sleeping with another boy of eight years pressing against my body and rolling around, kicking me in the side. In fact, I received a mere three hours of sleep, with my arms and feet dangling on the floor.

I welcomed the morning to come and the day to begin.

***

The next day they asked me to help clean the house. One of my cousins gave me a small broom that broke near the bottom. The only way to sweep was to bend over to the point that I touched my toes. I moved the broom across the floor, repeatedly sweeping the loose dirt toward the open door. Every speck of dust was swept at first, but as I progressed through the house, my back became sore from the constant bending. With weakened legs and my back feeling a sharp pain as if someone poked a long needle in my spine, I lowered to a crouching position and then sat on the ground, pushing dirt further ahead. I scooted toward the swept pile and continued to do this until I managed to shove dirt out of the home. At the beginning of my chore, I did a superb job; by the end, I missed many piles of dirt, but I didn't care. I just wanted to be done with the back-breaking labor. I am sure that the rest of the family noticed the house did not have the normal sparkling and dirt-free floors, but out of respect, they said nothing.

It wasn't long before we had grabbed our suitcases and made the long walk back to the bus station. We loaded a small van that was going direct to Homoine. The van soon took off, which allowed me to sleep with my head pressed against the glass with a light blow of the breeze from the driver's window, which opened wide.

As I exited the bus in our final destination, I looked around at the sights. Homoine, Mozambique, was a place that I will call home for the next few years.

A man stood by the bus stop with my father's name written on a piece of cardboard. They called him Father, as he worked in the church as pastor on Sundays. However, he worked in the hospital throughout the week. The reverend wasn't a doctor, as they had one man who served that role, but was a nurse and helped in whatever way the hospital needed.

The reverend was a short chubby man who wore a gentle smile and had a firm handshake as I noticed when he went through meeting everyone. Reverend Agostino had a shaven face, providing a respectable mien, and wore a necklace of the cross, noticeable for people to see. Dad told me that he was Mozambican but did speak English, which I welcomed with relief. I was getting tired of being clueless and giving off a fake smile as if I understood what was being said in this strange language. Sometimes people talked to me in the local tongue, and other times, they spoke to me in Portuguese. Mozambicans spoke multiple languages, but Portuguese had the distinction as being the official. It didn't matter which language they used: they blended and sounded the same, formulating an abstraction in which I was not ready to understand. When I found someone that spoke English, I felt proud to be able to have a conversation with him or her. The reverend, however, found more pleasure in speaking Portuguese with my father.

The reverend grabbed a few of the heavy bags that we had been lugging halfway across the country and walked with us to the new home. The reverend said that the house is near the hospital on the outskirts of the small town. We walked through a small section of the village and several small streets on the way to our new home.

The town had a small convenient store and a few bars but not much else that I could see. Most of the buildings had not been painted in years, and mud sprayed the bottom of each, which had no visible landscaping of flowers or trimmed trees. Many homes had torn and dented tin roofs with several large rocks placed on top to secure them in place. However, the town had a unique personality with people moving and selling goods on the side of the street. The town gave off a disposition of an old Western or ghostly deserted place, which yielded many adventures.

As we walked on a long dirt road through a few small alleyways and across a few backyards of people who worked toward cooking up a meal for the evening, we arrived at our small home.

The house was nothing extraordinary. It was a single rectangular shape. The roof had a single tin sheet, which covered the entire home. The brown walls were distinct and made of mud and cow dung, with interweaving sticks to give support. There were a few windows that I could see that had steel bars for protection.

The property looked freshly raked as the dirt had long streaks of creviced dirt. Grass was not to be seen in the front, except for a few single blades near the tall mango tree. Another small home sat on a different plot of land, around forty feet from the tree.

An older woman sat in front of the porch with a flameless fire, stirring a large pot of ncima, which was a staple food in Mozambique made from maize/cornflower. The woman stopped her daily chore and glared at us and didn't wave or bother to get up from where she sat and stared.

The priest showed us the shower room, which was outside with no running water. It had a small slab of concrete, tilted to offer drainage that allowed the water to stream outside. This would, of course, form a small puddle of mud. A few hooks attached to the walls so that clothes or a towel could dangle and not get dirty. The hooks were low-key and made of an old hanger and attached to a branch that was placed vertically to give support. The shower room was constructed out of reed material and woven in between many branches that lay parallel to each other and attached to four long sticks dug into the ground at each corner. This was a stopgap bathhouse, with no roof and four walls that would lean to one side at the slightest breeze. There was no door to the bathroom. You entered on the side and followed a curved path into the room, which provided the opening and privacy in place of a door. When I stood in the room, there were several holes in the assembled structure, which gave you little privacy during the day.

As I stood there, looking around, I wondered how they expected me to bathe with no showerhead or faucet with running water. The idea of standing naked—bathing in a room that could be tossed aside in the next natural disaster, exposing my privates for everyone to see—made me nauseous.

I smelled something that appeared to be waste. Walking out of the shower room, I noticed the small room continued into a separate place. I walked in, and there was a hole in the ground with flies swarming. As I walked closer, the stench grew more distinct; and as I approached to look through the hole, I realized that this was where I was to go to the bathroom. A hole in the ground lay where a toilet should sit, and around the inside of the outhouse, mud and pieces of paper were thrown in no particular place. I couldn't discern why paper rested in a bathroom, but upon closer examination, I realized that the paper was there to wipe your backside after performing your bathroom duties. A deep breath exited my mouth, and I closed my nose with my arm as I exited the room and walked closer to the mango tree.

The inside of the home sat vacant. There were two bedrooms, both not painted, and the floor made of hard cement. A sitting and dining room were connected. Around the back of the house, just outside the back door, another small building erected to form a small kitchen that had no electricity. With no electricity, stove, or proper cooking appliances, my mother needed to rely on starting fires and making our meal each night over burned coals. I wasn't sure how my mom was going to carry out cooking in this manner, being used to Western appliances.

When informed of this, her face became livid, maybe at the condition or at my father, but it was clear that she was mad. Mom loved to prepare food, and not being able to cook the way she knew how angered her. She liked to camp, so taking bucket baths outside or going to the outhouse was something that she could live with or learn to live with. But not being able to cook made her angry enough to start screaming at someone.

"Well . . . this way of living was good enough for me growing up, so it is good enough for us now," my father stated, trying to alleviate the tension that he sensed.

"Well, I will let your folks get unpacked, and I will be back here in an hour to show you the hospital," Father Agostino said. He walked away and didn't get but two feet before turning to face my father. "Oh, I will have people bring over a few more things. The church has a sofa, a table, and few cooking supplies to get you started until you can get a few more items."

"That would be great," my father said with a small smile emerging from his face.

***

I sat in the corner of my new room, which had nothing in it. There were no beds, closets, or night tables. There was one suitcase that had everything that I brought from the States. Before we left, a moving company was going to ship over our belongings and furniture. This would be a welcomed addition to the empty house, which echoed with every footstep and whisper.

What the reverend said kept coming up in my mind: "Unpack your things." I am not sure why I fixated on this simple task, except that I looked around, wondering how to do such a thing, without any place to put my clothes. As these words ran through my head, my nose started to run, and deep depression once again entered my small body. I hated myself for being so overwhelmed and weakened by such small and mundane things.

I could hear my mother, who was upset, talking with my father, but I couldn't make out what she was saying. I could have assumed that it was something to do with the kitchen. The sound of her voice did not comfort me; in fact, it made me sad because the anchor that held my emotions in check looked to be unraveling.

I heard two men outside arguing, which took my mind off the current argument. I rose to my feet and walked over to the small curtainless casement, which did not latch. Off in the distance, I saw two men standing a few inches from each other. Their hands were flailing in multiple directions. One person kept pointing in the distance and the other in the opposite direction. I couldn't understand them, but I started to assemble the words they should be saying. "We are going this way," "No, we are going this way," I said aloud as if in a nefarious Chinese movie. This brought on a slight smile, which curled upward toward my forehead. This smile relieved me, as I hadn't made one since the news.

"Aderito, let's go," my dad shouted from the living room.

My smile broke as I tore off my jeans and pulled on a pair of tan shorts that was on top of my suitcase. I rushed out of my room and through the small corridor into the dimly lit living room. A few men were bringing in a plastic table and a few plastic chairs. The reverend had a few brown reed mats rolled up and tucked under his arm.

"We call these esteira mats." He paused for a moment before continuing. "People here sit on them, and some folks sleep on them. You can use them until your beds arrive."

My mother gave a faint smile, which was more to be polite, not because of her excitement to receive a gift that was sure to give her back pains. She took the thin flimsy mats and rested them against the wall.

We stepped outside into the dimming sunset and waited for my father to lock the door before walking through the neighbor's front yard. The woman sat with her grandchildren in front of the porch, eating food with their hands. Taking the white ncima, she altered the contents into a ball, dipped it in a sauce that was placed on the side of the plate, and ate it. She continued to do this while we passed. The reverend greeted her in the local language, and they exchanged a few words. On several occasions, the reverend pointed in our direction as she nodded, curious at what he was saying. She gave a dazzling bright smile, which showed several teeth missing, and waved to us. She then clasped her hands together, clapped two times, and lowered her head.

I imagined that once she knew who we were and why we had moved next door, she was grateful for our presence. In unison, the three of us smiled and waved to her and her grandchildren who were preoccupied with their meal and less on the strangers.

We had to walk a few more minutes and around a sharp turn and then into a large compound. The building was white with a blue border around the bottom. There was a giant red cross over the main entrance. The box-shaped building looked small to be a hospital. There was a pleasant porch in front, and there were a few more buildings in the back of the main building.

We walked in, and the foul stench of near death hit me as if it were ready to knock me to the ground. As we turned around the corner, there was a long row of benches, where several people were sitting with their heads between their legs. I couldn't decide if they were sick or in the pre-mourning stages. We walked through this long corridor, and in each room, I saw more sick people. I stopped in front of the room at the end of the corridor. I looked in and saw a juvenile shirtless young man. He had a large gash across his stomach. Blood was spewing out under the bandage that covered his entire abdomen. His stomach rose and fell to the beat of his heart, and his head tilted back as far as it could be stretched. The man's teeth clenched together, and he was forcing himself not to throw out a scream. His hands held the bed, and I could see the veins in his forearms and the sweat form around his body, drenching the dirty, stained bed. The man's body trembled as he raised his head and looked over in my direction. Fear manifested in his eyes as he dreaded his fate.

I sensed loneliness in his longing gaze. His head lowed to the pillow as he started to pray to the ceiling, as if he were succumbing to his fate, asking for forgiveness and acceptance into the heavens.

A nurse noticed me glaring at the boy and rushed over to close the door. The window into the room was covered with a small poster that left half the glass exposed. This allowed me to continue to stare at what appeared to others as a closed door. In the small crack, I saw the women walk toward the man with a needle erected toward his leg. Her backside covered the injection; but when she had moved, revealing the man once more, he looked relaxed and content with his destiny.

I looked around and realized that my parents had left. I rushed out the back door and into a large open place with several other buildings that were consultation rooms to work with AIDS victims as well as expecting mothers.

The compound had benches with people surrounding them. Nurses walked around, and people conversed as they waited for their loved ones to be released. It was obvious who was waiting for someone who had been sick and who waited for someone who wasn't. Many people laughed while others hung their heads low toward the ground and sat in silence, contemplating the day's or week's events.

Outside, there were little landscaped patches. There were a few sections of grass, but for the most part, the hospital had nothing but dirt that kicked up with the wind. Off in the distance, there sat an isolated bush that had bright red and pink flowers blooming and there were a few trees, including one mango that provided shade for the guests and patients to take cover during the afternoon sun.

We walked around the outside for a few minutes. The reverend told my parents that they would work with wounded victims from the civil war as well as with the sick.

As we walked back through the buildings, I saw one room with a row of beds, one right after another, with no privacy. Occupying each bed was a small child. Many didn't look sick while other had bandages covering their heads and limbs. I walked into the room, and the first child whom I noticed was a teenage girl who had lost her arm. Her face was sullen, and her back leaned against the bedframe, wearing civilian clothes. She looked at me, and I couldn't utter a single word because I didn't know what I could say. Her faded look said help, but I did nothing, except offer her the only thing I could think of: a smile. I raised my hand above my waist and waved to her before turning around and walking out of the room through the long corridor and back out the front entrance, where my parents waited.

The rest of the evening, I spent at the reverend's house, who was amiable enough to make us dinner.

Once dinner finished, we made the short walk home, soon walking into the dimly lit chamber. We laid out our mats and lay together as a family in the sitting room of our empty cement-floored house. We didn't have blankets yet, so we snuggled up next each other and slept in our clothes that we wore during the day. I fell asleep to the sounds of my mother's heart beating on my back.

CHAPTER 4

The next few weeks, I sat secluded in my bedroom. The depression, environment, and new experience of being petrified and fortified of the outside world left many sleepless nights. I was scared to leave the house because there were so many unknowns. There was an unknown language, people, culture, sickness, and conflict. This scared me to the point that each night I went to bed terrified, and many nights, I slept with my parents for the sense of security. These few weeks, I came out to eat, bathe, and then go back into the house to stare at the blank walls that got smaller, trapping my life and mind into the dim, bleak routine.

As I woke up in a hurry, I rubbed my eyes and listened to the rooster outside. He fit into my daily routine by giving me a prompt reminder every morning. The rooster woke up and walked straight to the bedroom, where I lay agitated, to deliver his calls. Lifting my blanket, I pushed it to the side and then rose from my mat, which I had been used to sleeping on the last few weeks, and walked out of the room. As I looked from side to side, I tried to collect my thoughts and balance and scanned the house to see who was around, but no one was present. Mom and Dad should be at home today, waiting for our container to arrive from the States. A TV, which would run off a car battery, and other amenities should arrive to help pass the time. For three weeks, I slipped into my old routine of staring into nothingness using my mind and the colorless walls to occupy my thoughts. Yet it was different with no distraction or people to occasionally lift me from the depth of my imagination; simply put, I was bored out of my mind, sitting at the house, with nothing but time to occupy my thoughts. The sight of my belongings would be a fresh reminder of childhood.

I walked into the exterior kitchen where our maid sat, boiling water.

Dad hired someone to help pack the water, cook, and clean to relieve my mother of her daily chores and allow her to help in the hospital. In the States, we never had a maid because we could never afford one. Dad was making less money in Mozambique, but because the cost of labor was so cheap, we were able to afford these luxuries.

There was no running water in the house, so the maid had to fetch some in a water point half a mile away. Dulce did this every day. She also cleaned and prepared our meals.

"Olá, Dulce," I greeted her in Portuguese. I hadn't learned much, but I did learn a few basic greetings. Dad began to speak the language in the household in hopes that my mother and I absorbed something. So far, it was working but frustrating at the same time because it was hard for me to convey my thoughts and feelings in a language that I had just started to understand basic conversational skills. I was, for the most part, resisting the words, which was more out of defiance. School was going to start in a few weeks, so I knew that if I was going to survive in this environment and meet new friends, I should start to study hard.

Dulce was a petite woman in her early thirties. The soft-spoken maid had an abundance of patience, which was shown in her unrushed and leisurely pace in life. Dulce's short hair and skinny arms, which were one size away from being grotesquely anorexic, added to her sad figure. Dulce was a humorless woman who experienced such darkness, which made it impossible to experience joy. Dulce's darkened eyes had bags under them, and they lay drooping toward the ground, afraid of the deep connection of other humans.

She sat on a small stool that was a foot above the ground and knees raised toward her chest and her arms outstretched toward the embers, poking them with a long stick. A kettle perched on top of a steel-framed box, over the fire, with water that just started to boil.

"Would you like to take a bath?" she stated in Portuguese, trying to reduce the speed in which she spoke to help my lack of understanding.

Yes was the usual response as I watched her pour hot boiling water into a two-gallon black bucket with a thin metal handle. Dulce took water stored in a plastic five-gallon yellow container and poured that into the bucket, making the water warm. I grabbed the bucket and a plastic cup that was sitting in the corner of the kitchen propped on a plastic chair that acted as a multipurpose table. With the necessary bathing equipment in hand, I made my way to the small bathhouse.

When I walked outside, I looked around to see which of the neighbors were roaming around, completing the daily chores. I was looking nervously for women, but no one was present. The nervous energy was imminent every time I had to step outside to bathe because anyone could walk around and peek through the various holes placed sporadically around the small room.

When I entered the shower, I took a deep breath and then one more look around the room. Dad had made a small ledge where soap could sit, but other than this, the bathroom sat the same. I disrobed and stood in the bitter morning for a few seconds. A slight wind conquered my backside, which sent shivers up the front of my body. I grabbed the green cup and dipped it into the warm water and raised it above my head to empty on my back and then again on my front, allowing the water to drip to the cement flooring and out the drain.

As I reached for the soap, I looked forward where I saw two little beady eyes peering through one of the holes. My hands cupped my privates, and I yelled for her to leave, but she didn't. The young girl only managed to giggle to herself as she looked at one hand cupping my genitals and the other hand wrapping around my backside. With my knees bent, my whole body tightened to try to bring myself dignity. I shivered, more out of fright and less from morning cold.

I knew this child as one of the grandchildren who lived next door and who had been curious ever since I moved into the small house. I didn't dare continue washing as long as she surveyed, waiting my move. More shouting pursued for her to leave. "Deixar, deixar," I kept squealing yet got nothing but a tiny giggle from a five-year-old. This could have been because my pronunciation was off, but more than likely, it was because her curiosity outweighed the demands of an older boy.

Standing naked and vulnerable, in the now-warming air, I yelled some more but was powerless toward the small girl. Vulnerability makes you weak, even to the smallest and least threatening of people. Catching people in a state of such weakness is a powerful tool toward controlling the human reactions. The young girl might not have understood this, but deployed it with precision.

The grandmother called for her to come, and she rose to her feet. As if the commander's threatening voice reigned down upon her, the girl was gone. Fear was replaced with relief, and my heartbeat slowed down and became steady again. I gulped loud and raised my eyes to the sky, to be met by a strong beam from the sun, drying my water-beaded body. Several deep breaths exhaled, and I quickly continued the lathering of soap.

The suds soon covered my body, and just as I reached down for the plastic cup to rinse, a noise came from the distance. A chicken clucked and pecked its way, searching for the endless amounts of food it consumed. As it turned the corner, its eyes rolled back, exposing the bright whites. I spoke under my breath, annoyed at the creature that bore no intelligence yet won a pivotal mind game.

First, a little girl won the battle, now a mindless chicken. I wasn't going to have it. I was fed up! Mad at the world, and this chicken needed to be the brunt of my anger. I plotted the revenge on the bird that showed up at the wrong time. Fed up, I took my foot back, ready to kick. The only outcome could be the chicken flying over the makeshift wall, out of the bathroom, and across the dirt yard. An image of the outcome already played in my head, and it sounded so perfect.

As I swung forward, the slippery concrete took control. My two feet went out toward the sky, and I landed on my back. The limbs of my body rested on the cement slab with my feet dangling in the dirt. I raised my head and found the chicken still standing in front, fixated on my defeat. The image I placed on this moment and the significance of regaining dignity were overshadowed by the indulgence of humiliation. Being defeated by a young girl, who had barely learned to walk, and now by the lowest of intelligent creatures was summing up my three weeks in Africa. The ability to hold my pride in check and learn to be humble in each lesson. Of course, as a child, I didn't see these moments as lessons. I saw them as annoyances.

As I looked around, I found a small half-buried rock in the dirt next to the side of the concrete. I gripped the rock and heaved it toward the chicken. The bird jumped and fluttered its wings toward the reed wall of the bathroom but stopped short of exiting through the opened holes. Soon, the animal controlled its emotions and once again stood in the dirt path and continued to search for food, as if the beating did not affect him.

The bath was soon finished with the chicken's eyes going from me to the food and back again. Upon my exit and dressing in last night's clothes, I said sarcastically with my arms stretched wide, "Did you have a nice show?"

I dressed and decided that I should explore the village. After three weeks, trapped in my emotions, I finally realized that the troubles did not disappear with moping around the house or a night's sleep. Few people cared to hear my troubles or were willing to take the time to comfort and nurse my depression.

I walked outside and up the long stretch of dirt road. Children ran, women cooked, and men sat on the porches having deep conversations regarding something significant in their lives. Life, by outside appearances, moved seamlessly in peace, as if the troubles of the war were not relevant. Was this the daily life that I was destined to lead? Was there a need to succumb to my fear and cower in the corner? Were they unaware of the war that could change their lives? Or did they come to the realization that a war can define their actions and daily lives or they can define themselves despite the violence?

I entered a small path barely big enough for a car to drive. This route took me through a long steep trail into the valley. As I walked deeper into the dense-tree-covered landscape, the walking path got smaller and smaller to the extent that it vanished.

Off into the distance, I heard a sweet subtle shriek. This stopped me in my current course. The shriek of a young lady sounded as if she was hurt and crying out for someone to help. A few more yells proceeded to follow, and the horror of a single squeal turned into a series of playful yells mixed with giggles. I listened to the playful sounds for a few seconds. Sounds of laughter mixed with the sounds of children running through water, jumping and splashing in a reckless and pleasing manner.

As I approached the sounds, a small river appeared; that moved peacefully downstream with children playing nearby, without a care in the world. I couldn't help but think of the people wounded in the hospital, the constant stream of military vehicles passing by, and other vehicles of young men hanging out with machetes and AK-47s flung in the air in a pointless attempt at fear.

A few hundred feet up the hill, problems plagued the country; but here, watching children my age playing made me smile and realize that, under the surface of cruelty, there may be hope. I sat on the ground, just hidden behind the wilderness staring hypnotically at the children while smiling. I wanted to move forward and play, but something held me back.

A young boy took off, running several hundred feet to tackle another boy to the ground. The boys rolled in the hard soil. The soil they rolled in stuck to their wet bodies, and they continued on their path until they rolled into the river. I wanted to join but didn't know how I was going to start the interaction.

My eyes turned from the wrestling boys to an adolescent girl, my age, off in the distance. She was skipping in the water as her arms were flying in a wild motion. A beaming smile that stretched across her face brightened the day, as her soft sweet voice sang a song, but I wasn't sure what the words were. As she skipped, water splashed over her head, soaking her clothes. She took a seat in the water and allowed the low-flowing river to cascade over her legs, soaking the bottom half of her body.

I wasn't sure why I felt the way that I did, but this was the most spectacular person I had ever seen. The girl was gaunt with long wavy hair. Her skin was soft and glimmered in the hot sun. The high cheekbones allowed dimples to form when she smiled at her carefree actions.

A young boy saw me hiding being the bushes. The boy walked over and said a bunch of words, in Portuguese. I didn't understand what he was saying, but he kept repeating "Americano," in which I replied, "sim." I didn't know the boy, but he heard that I was from America. I think the word had gotten around that I was living in the village; and when he saw a different boy, although looking the same, sitting before him, he made an educated guess as to who I was.

"Victoria, venha cá," the boy shouted. The young girl that was sitting in the water lifted her knees toward her chest and, with the strength of her legs and the help of her arms, lifted herself to a vertical position, and walked over to where the majority of children now gathered. "Ela fala Inglês," the boy stated.

Victoria approached and saw me sitting on the hard dirt with my feet buried. She didn't have to ask, as she knew who I was. "Are you American?" she said in a shy voice, shriveling her body, not wanting to speak English in front of her friends.

"Do you speak English?" I asked, shocked at the few words that she managed to say.

"A little," she said in a low tone.

The other children giggled and then went back to playing in the water. She sat beside me, and we carried out a quick conversation. The English wasn't good, but she managed to mention a few things. I found out that she had learned from a nun who worked in the church and Victoria had lived in Homoine her whole life.

"Come, let play," Victoria said, trying to find the right words to express her wish.

I ran with her, away from the other children, and landed into the shallow river. The two of us awkwardly splashed for several minutes until we both got tired. Victoria and I found a spot under a tree to offer shade. The emotions I felt were foreign, but the connection was strong. The subtle beams of sunlight flowing through the various patches in the trees made me hope the moment would never pass. The quick conversation covered everything, from school to life and family. Laughter filled the air on several occasions and a serious tone on a few more, but we often found ourselves experiencing awkward silence.

I sat up as she was explaining her family to me. I looked deep into her eyes, and nothing she said registered, as I was intent on her simplicity and flicker within her presence. As I stared into her dark eyes, I could think of nothing but the thoughts and feelings that rushed through my head. I couldn't connect with it; it was not like anything I had ever experienced.

Many girls talked to me in the States, mostly because they were forced to, but none made my emotions flutter the way she did. I had shivers throughout my body, yet the sun was shining. My stomach tightened, and my palms were sweaty, yet I wasn't sick. I didn't know if the feelings were normal or if they would pass.

Victoria must have sensed my foolish behavior, staring hypnotically at the young girl. The sounds of the river faded, the noises of the children muted, and no words entered my thoughts, only the faint whispers within my head.

A young boy came from behind with a handful of dirt and crept within inches off my back. Before Victoria could inform me of my fate, the soil landed on my head and trickled to my shoulder toward my lap. The dry hot sand woke me from my reverie and shocked me back into reality.

I am not sure what came over me, but I jumped to my feet and chased after him. The young boy ran fast through the dirt before finding, off in the distance, a friend whom he grabbed with both hands and placed him in front, acting as a shield. I reached to the ground and flicked dirt up toward both boys, forcing them to shield their eyes and face from the flying particles. The children waited for the slightest pause on my part before they kicked sand toward me, hitting me below the waist.

Laughter soon followed as I ran toward the water, hoping to be shielded by the rushing stream, but the chase continued. The young boy leaped toward my back and landed on both shoulders, forcing me to fall to my knees. The trajectory of my body falling soon propelled me to my stomach, submersing my body underwater for a few seconds. I could faintly hear the laughter of the boy as he straddled my body. The playful fighting continued as I turned around, looking at his wide grin. I grabbed his shoulder and turned him over so that I was now overpowering him. My hand reached into the water, and I splashed large amounts into his face and continued to do so until the other boy came from behind and started splashing water toward the both of us.

As we played, off in the distance, a gunshot rang and echoed through the woods. Another one followed, and then a series of bullets pursued. We stopped, rose to our feet, stared at each other, and then looked up the long hill in silence. The shooting soon stopped, but the ringing of gunfire stayed in my ear. I didn't know if I should run up the hill or if I should stay. The thought of my mother and father being injured or hurt lingered in my mind, as I wasn't sure of the intentions of the firing. The shots could have been directed toward someone, or the soldiers were shooting off their guns into the air in a fit of rage.

Happiness escaped, and fear entered. The peacefulness of the day's events passed, and the harsh reality of the world away from the river came flooding in, and I could think of nothing else but the dark sounds of the guns ringing throughout the valley and the fear the people must have felt.

The children waited for half an hour before, without any preconceived idea or warning, they started to tear up the hill as if they had a hunch that the men with guns had left. Time to scope out the damage and make sure that the families were okay. Victoria grabbed my hand and pulled me along. During the shooting and after, my feet and entire body went numb; and when she grabbed me by the hand, my legs didn't walk. But once the recognition and shock left, the only thing I could think of was my family. I felt that the children understood the dangers, and yet they still ran up the hill. Even though I just met them, I felt protected, and so I ran beside them. My feet began to pound in a strange rhythmic bold pattern. There were deranged emotions that I had never felt. There was this sense of fear that hovered around me. I think it was fear for my life as well as my families. Yet covering the fear was this strange sense of heroism sweeping into the village with my friends ready to fight and willing to sacrifice my life for a greater purpose.

We reached the edge of the road just before entering the village. The other children hid behind a line of bushes to scope out the land. I stood erect, wondering what they were doing. Would I have to continue our epic deed by myself? Let us see what has happened, how we can help. Confusion started, and thoughts raced through my mind when reality struck, and Victoria yanked me by the hand with enough force to knock me to my knees. I think they may have been smarter, willing to cower behind a bush to ensure security. In the act of war, a hero that stands to live another day is better than a foolish man who runs into a battle blinded by his own sense of epic being.

We sat behind a bush, trembling with fear as we saw an average pickup truck turn a corner and head toward us. The driver had his hand dangling from the truck. The man gazed in our direction as if he saw the once-brave kids trembling behind the bushes, but he did nothing. In the back of the truck were men, each with AK-47s in one hand and a machete in the other. Some men had their weapons drawn in the air while others satisfied their anger with yelling and screaming. One man sat on the cab of the truck while another had one leg in and one out, sitting on the tailgate. One person looked over, but he didn't see us, but the mask he wore was that of darkness. The man's eyes squinted in the falling sun, and his face squished together. In his right hand, he held the gun tight, and I could see his veins bulge out from his forearm.

As the truck passed, my eyes glued on the man. The man raised his AK-47 and pointed it in our direction. The man held it there for a second. Could he see us? I looked at his dark eyes and saw his right eye wink at the gang and me. Trepidation made my body wobble, and I fell backward to land on the rocky path. My mouth widened, and my chest and stomach ached of pain. My body shook as I saw the man show off a half smile. The smile was mischievous, one that resonated in my memory for many days to come. The man lowered the gun and did nothing. I watched as the car turned another corner and sped up toward the setting sun. We stayed in that spot, watching the truck get smaller and smaller until it vanished.

People began to emerge from their homes. We got up and ran toward the chaos of others. I pushed and jabbed my way through the crowd, with Victoria by my side. There were three young men lying in a pool of their own blood. Their eyes turned back, revealing the eerie whites. Their bodies were lifeless, and I stood saddened, frightened, and scared to see the sight but relieved that no one I knew was among the young men lying in the middle of the open yard.

Several men stepped forward and grabbed the body that lay closest to where I stood. As they raised the body, the arms rested toward the ground. The head flung backward, and blood dripped from the skull. The young man's body lay limp, and off in the distance, a woman was held back, but her screams hung in the air. The woman's body flew to the ground, and she let out loud bellows as she pounded her thighs. Tears flew from the eyes and soaked the ground below, creating a small pool of water, turning her world into mud.

Standing, watching the person carried away and the woman distraught because she had lost someone, made me ashamed because just a few minutes before I was glad that the man was not my father.

These men had someone who loved them, and although I eventually went home relieved, someone in the small village had to have a home filled with sadness. I realized at that moment that no winners could be declared in a war.

I couldn't help but wonder what the man had done to deserve a termination of such brutal ferocity. What was his crime? Did he commit a sin punishable by death?

The men were carried away from the ground one by one. Men and women cried and pounded the earth as they grieved in the only way they knew how. Those who weren't friends or family of the deceased stood in silence, heads lowered to the ground, not daring to be the first to speak. The last man was carried away, and now we stood in silence, looking at the deep dark pool of red blood that soaked up into the ground. The brutal remains of such destruction and violence sat just a few feet away.

A single tear rolled down my cheek and hung on my chin for a few seconds before falling to the ground. Victoria must have seen this as she reached for my hand and grabbed it, holding it near her body. Victoria's soft hands felt comforting to me. I held her hand for several minutes before the crowd dispersed, leaving us to watch the thick blood spread outward and soak into the ground, where it stayed until the next rainfall.

CHAPTER 5

My mother's deepest fears were starting to become into the saddest reality. Appalled at what I saw a few days ago, she had a strong overbearing presence. She battled with the alienable right of a child being allowed the freedom to explore, and my safety. The safety, of course, overshadowed any right I felt I had. As a result, I was confined to the hospital where she and my father could see me or at home, where Dulce kept a watchful eye.

This was an enthralling turn of events; just a few days ago, I closed the door to my scared thought of leaving home and locked myself in my bedroom. Now I only thought of the outside world and going to the river. I felt connected, safe, and drawn to the peaceful tranquility of the land as I had so much fun with Victoria that I wanted it back. This, of course, didn't matter because Victoria came over every day. Not much was done, but it was gratifying to keep her company.

The rebel group, RENAMO, showed up every midmorning. The soldiers didn't do much, just patrolled. I think they were trying to scare us and sweep the countryside, working toward a mission that was, of course, unbeknownst to the village. They usually shook their guns, screamed at a few people, and stole food and gas. The men left an hour later and caused little damage to the people and no casualties. I never understood the reasons for their behavior, except an inconvenience to the town. It always made me scared because you never knew what the mission or goals were. Victoria and I never knew if they planned to kill someone or just take things. In any regard, they affected our lives, and I hated them for this.

Victoria and I were sitting under the mango tree, enjoying a light snack while talking about school. Victoria was trying to explain what might happen at the local school. Based on what she was saying, I was starting to have a few anxiety attacks. I couldn't imagine going to a place where they beat kids to adjust their behavior.

Off in the distance, a subtle rumble of an engine rang in our ears. The sound appeared to be getting closer to the house. This was the intimation that people should leave the streets. Victoria and I leaped to our feet and ran inside the house. We went through our usual prep work, which my mom and dad told us to do. Victoria and I locked the front and back doors and went around to each window to make sure that they were locked and the curtains drawn.

Mom and Dad told us to sit on the floor and play cards or something until they left. However, there was too much curiosity in our young bodies. We went to the couch, positioned under the casement. We kneeled on the hard surface, which made our heads at the perfect height to watch out the window. I pulled a small corner of the curtain back so that most of my head was covered except for my eyes, which peeked out the casement. Victoria did the same thing on the other side of the curtain.

Victoria and I had to wait a few minutes before we saw the truck pass. It was the RENAMO troops. These soldiers were the same group who came that terrible day, which had forced me to have many nights lying awake, fearful of a return. Every time I saw them, my body shivered. I feared the man who smiled at us as I saw the dark devilish grin in my memory. The troubled darkened demeanor in his presence was felt, and I couldn't help but shudder with the thought of his return.

I didn't dare speak, even though they were far enough that hearing us would be impossible. Our eyes glued outside, as I couldn't keep from watching the scene unfold. My curiosity for the truth took over my rational thinking as I needed an answer to my burning questions. By watching them off in the distance, that meant they weren't close enough to attack or harm the people in my house. I never wanted to be surprised by the possible ambush. Therefore, keeping a close eye on the truck and the men who occupied it meant that I would never be forced to face them without a fighting chance.

The truck stopped several hundred feet away. The soldiers disembarked the vehicle except the driver who continued to sit in his car with his arm lying limp, pressed against the door. The men held their guns to their chests, and their eyes passed from house to house. They stood like this for several minutes before they spread out.

The same person who appeared to point his gun at us grabbed a woman from one of the neighborhood houses. I didn't know her well, but Victoria introduced her to me as Claudia. He dragged her by the hair back to the vehicle. The man appeared to have no remorse as he yelled at her, trying to pull away. Every time she pulled back, the man shook her forward. Soon, the tremendous power and the impact of her body being wrenched forced her legs to give in and follow her captor. They arrived at the truck, and the man flung her whole body forward. Claudia's back hit the metal of the vehicle hard, and whip lashed her head backward toward the steel beast, where her head hit, creating a small dent. She landed on her knees and wept toward the ground.

Claudia was a strong woman, who once wore a splendid face that was now covered in stress. Her eyes had bright bags under them, and her face blotted with darker spots and scars from the various times she had been beaten or injured from the tough life of an African woman in the middle of a war. The strength left her, and she was now weakened, weeping on her knees toward the men to spare her life.

Following behind her was her husband, Custodio, being dragged by two other men. Custodio screamed loud in the air and kicked his feet forward. Custodio wrestled his shoulders back and forth, trying to shove his heels into the ground and stop the forward movement, but the strength of the men overpowered the drive and determination for freedom.

Claudia's husband was tossed beside her, and now the two held hands side by side on their knees as several men towered over. One person was yelling, but I heard nothing.

"What are they going to do?" I asked, anxious for a quick answer.

"I don't know," Victoria replied.

"What are they saying?"

"Don't know."

"What did they do?"

"Probably nothing . . . but support FRELIMO government."

I was worried as I needed answers, yet none sufficed my inquisitiveness for the truth. I couldn't keep from looking at the brutal violence. The thought of me staring out the window at something you thought only happened in the movies felt exciting and terrifying. I did this because I couldn't understand the barbarism and the ferocious acts of violence toward other humans. This made me sick, yet I couldn't stop looking at it.

One person raised his hand to the sky and came with force on the woman's head, catapulting her to tumble to the ground before being propped back up by another onlooker. At the sight of the blow, Victoria lowered her body and curled up on the couch. Victoria grabbed her knees and placed them against her chest. She rocked back and forth and hummed to herself, trying to think of happier times and not on what was happening a few feet from where she lay. She might have seen this before, and she could foretell what was to come next, but it was hard to tell as she didn't speak of things that caused her emotional pain.

Another man lowered his gun, walked behind a large tree, and rolled out a tree stump that the local villagers made use of for cutting firewood. He placed it in front of the man. Custodio shook his head and screamed. This was the first time that the strong man kneeled, visibly shaken. His tears were not of sadness but of fear. Custodio must have known his fate.

The man who grabbed the trunk walked over to Custodio on his knees. The soldier tried to grab his hand, but he resisted. A swift blow to his head by a strong fist was the one thing that could receive his obedience. Custodio went tumbling to the ground and found his sweaty body lying with his face resting on the dirt, with his butt sticking in the air. A soldier grabbed his arm, dragged his body ten feet in the dirt, and placed his arm on the stump.

The man whom I feared moved forward. He had a long scar that stretched from his ear to his eye and still carried the iniquitous smile of a man who had no morals or feelings toward humans. I had yet to see him carry out the cruelty I knew was deep within. However, looking at him, I knew that something wasn't right and that he might have been born an evil man sent to cause trepidation on his own country. The man grabbed Custodio's arm and held it on top of the splintering stump.

Custodio's legs flew and kicked violently, which made holding his arm in place imminently difficult. The man with the scar nodded to a colleague, who came over and kicked Custodio several times on his stomach. This forced him to lie limp, weep, and grab his body, but subtly moving, fearful of the ceaseless attack that may pursue.

Custodio continued to weep as the man returned with a machete and stood over his broken heart. Custodio's arm held to the stump while the machete raised high in the air and then came with massive force. The slash had broken skin, exposing the wet flesh of his muscles. Blood rushed out, spewing high into the air. With each blow of the machete landing on his flesh and bone, the man's yells grew louder and louder until he could only weep. The soldier didn't slow and each time tore more muscle and released more blood until he reached the bone. Through the yells, screams, and pleas, the man showed no mercy. Once the arm was severed, Custodio fell to the ground and raised the section of the arm that was left. Blood dripped from his arm, ran through his shirt, and exited to the ground. The man with the scar took the other half of his arm and threw it onto Custodio's chest as a stark reminder of his punishment. Custodio, once strong and noble, lay broken with deafening yells of agony that echoed around the village. As he looked at his arm, the loss of the blood and the terror that took over his body were too much; and Custodio went silent, resting his head on the blood-soaked ground, and eventually passed out.

The man whom I feared most grabbed the woman. He lowered the machete to her face. Claudia shook at the sight of the rusted blade pressed next to her eye. Sweat formed and dripped, and tears soon followed as she clenched her lips together, trying not to scream. He grabbed her shirt and cut the ratty and dirty cloth in half, exposing her breast. Claudia rested on her knees, not daring to look at his face. Her body shrank, and her fists clenched together. I hoped that she could find the strength to take a whack at the man, but that meant an immediate death. Claudia appeared to think it but didn't dare make the valiant feat.

He reached his hand to her face and caressed her cheek. The machete lowered, and he grabbed her chin, pulling it toward his body so that he saw her face. He looked in her eyes and must have seen panic but did not flinch. Her mouth was released, and her face went limp once again as she lowered her head to the side. The man grabbed her breast hard and rubbed it back and forth. Claudia gasped and clenched her body, hoping that it would cease. The man gained such pleasure from playing with the woman's soul and the trepidation that it caused her.

Claudia looked into his eyes, trying to face the individual and not allow perturbation to enter her body. The women, out of an attempt to thwart the rebel, spit into his status as one last heroic act of defiance. He raised his hand high to his face and slapped her hard before pushing her head back toward the truck.

His hand reached for her breast, and he held on tight. The man lowered the machete and paused, pressing the blade into her skin, hard enough to create a reaction but soft enough to keep it from breaking through releasing her blood. The machete pressed harder, and he started to cut into the skin. Claudia screamed and tried to move away, but two men grabbed her from behind and held her in place. The man continued to carve slower, trying to prolong the agony. He ignored her cries and pleas to stop, and he continued. I could see the wish in his eyes and maybe a sick satisfaction of causing pain to an innocent woman.

Cutting the right breast off looked similar to cutting the turkey at Thanksgiving. The man sliced back and forth fastidiously. This man did not look like a rookie butcher—he had done this before—and by the sheer delectation in his presence, I knew this wasn't going be the last. He made his way through the entire piece of meat and then held it high into the air, as if he performed a barbaric rite of passage, celebrating an insane victory that I never was able to comprehend.

The piece was held tight in his hands, dripping blood through his fingers. The man drowned out the weeps and cries of the woman who sat limp next to him and held the breast toward his head. He pretended to lick it as if he were mocking or imitating the eating of meat. The motion was repeated several times before taking it and throwing it back into the woman's face. This hit her, smearing blood across the cheek before landing on the ground. The women lowered her head and looked at the space that once held her womanhood. Claudia rested her buttocks on her ankles and gasped, raising and lowering her chest. She convulsed and fell to the ground and crawled forward so that she lay next to her husband. Claudia rested her head on his legs and panted as she tried to come to grips with the senseless pain that she had endured for unclear reasons.

The towering men, dressed in green military uniforms, loaded the truck. The man with the scar continued to loom over the two, clenching his teeth and then spitting in their direction, spraying them with his spittle. The man loaded in the back of the truck, and within seconds, they turned around and sped off toward the house.

As the truck came closer to my house, I lowered my head and sat next to Victoria. I placed my hand on her back and rubbed it as gently as I could, trying to soothe her as she wept. Victoria continued to rock back and forth. My mouth and eyes widened as I pondered the images for a while, but the right words to describe them were never found.

Dulce rushed through the house and out the front door to help the two get to the hospital.

"It's over," I said.

"Did they do it?" Victoria said in a simple innocent tone.

I nodded yes. The two of us sat in silence, not knowing what to say to contemplate the events or put our minds at ease.

Dulce came back into the house a few hours later, covered in blood. Dulce's clothes drenched, and minimal trickles of blood dripped from her fingers. She had dried blood caked to her knee, just below the brown dress that she wore, which was blotted with red spots. She looked at us, still sitting on the couch. "Some people just don't know how to be decent," she said as her lower lip trembled. There was nothing else that was to be said. Dulce walked into the kitchen and sat, beginning to cry. Victoria grabbed my hand and held it toward her body.

CHAPTER 6

Victoria and I sat across from each other, listening to the quiet flow of the river. Wind continued to come from the south, batting around her hair and the soft ground beside our feet. It blew around in circles, spreading small particles of dirt. The bright sun exposed our legs while the shade of the trees shielded our bodies from the warm sun.

The secluded section of the river felt safe. I didn't suspect members of RENAMO coming with guns as the river provided the perfect shelter and protection. The only time I was apprehensive was when I made the long tiring walk up the hill and back to the village. There were always the unknown people who might be waiting behind any bush or corner.

"Why do people fight?" I asked, trying to make small talk and find answers to my many questions.

"Don't know. Mozambique has been fighting for a long time," Victoria said with her head lowered. "Maybe it's just a way of life. Why did you move here?"

"I don't know. Maybe my dad wanted to go back to Mozambique and help people. His brother still lives here, in Maxixe, and he wanted to be closer . . . the church in the States had a relationship with the church here, which is why we ended up here."

There was serene quietude as I dug a stick into the ground, creating a gaping hole. Victoria stood up and started to walk toward the river. She stuck her foot in the water and splashed the large toe around, trying to discern the water's temperature. I got up and walked over to where she stood. I tried to walk lightly so that she didn't hear, hoping to pull a playful prank. Once I was a few feet away, I pushed hard on her upper back. Victoria tripped on a large rock and went headfirst into the water, soaking her clothes, which now filled and rippled with the subtle flow of water. Victoria turned around so that her face popped up from the water. At first, her eyes squinted and mouth bunched together. Victoria wiped her face clean of water and scowled into my eyes. Victoria's hands propped her body in an upward position and stayed like this for several seconds, appearing by countenance to be angry.

Recoiling backward, I thought that I crossed the line. Before reaching a place of safety, Victoria jumped out of the water. Her clothes were clung tight to her body, and water dripped back into the river. Her shoulders broadened and head lowered, yet Victoria's eyes fixated on me in the distance. Victoria looked like a bull ready to make her attack, with flaring nostrils and protruding eyes. Her shoulders rose and fell, and the breathing became heavy.

Victoria started to walk out of the water, with her legs spread wide, arms and muscles flexing. Her dark eyes squinted to intimidate and send a message, which worked. The long strides soon blended into a jog before entering into a progressive run, splashing water and creating small ripples.

Victoria ran with tremendous force through the dirt. I stood frozen in place because I enjoyed watching her run. But was terrified of what may happen. When she was just a few feet away, a small soft laughter filled the scene. Panic escaped, and reassurance took over as I broke into a slight smile as my body shivered with warmth and anxiety. I dodged to the right just as Victoria lunged forward, missing by an inch. As she managed to gather her composure, the pursuant chase continued.

Victoria and I chased around the sand, back into the water, and then back out; and soon, she cornered me against a tree, where I found myself trapped. Victoria pounced, as I tried to run away, but managed to grab my wrist. I thought breaking free could be possible, but with incredible force, Victoria pulled hard and my body lunged backward. She grabbed my shoulders and gave a fierce bear hug. For a strange reason, being caught was comforting.

Victoria soon let go, and the chase continued, this time toward the river. She was close behind. As the river approached, two strong hands pressed against my back and then pushed toward the river. My body flew forward, and I slipped on a rock, heading toward the water. Before my hands could get underneath, my head hit the cold water, followed by the rest of my body. My head submerged for a few seconds as water rushed over. Turning around, Victoria stood on the shore, laughing, as I lay helpless, exposing my head. Victoria jumped in and landed on top, pushing my head further into the water. My arms flew out, trying to gain a solid grip. My right hand found her shoulder. With one last attempt to gain control, I pushed hard toward the shore and managed to twist her over so that I was now on top.

The force of this roll allowed her to gain momentum, and we rolled several more times upstream until finishing with me on top. I rose to my feet and ran upstream with her trailing. I stopped, trying to catch my breath. Trying to avoid another tackle, I reached my hands into the water and splashed large quantities toward her face. This stopped the forward momentum and forced Victoria to cower away, holding her hands up, blocking the splashing water. During a brief break, she managed to gather composure and proceeded to reciprocate the splashing. Each gathering large scoops of water and pushing toward the other, creating large splashes that traveled high into the air and submersed our bodies. The laughter traveled and echoed through the valley; yet we consumed the time with laughter, jovial play, and less with what other might hear or say.

Soon, getting tired, we sat near the shore, with legs resting in the water, allowing it to rush over our lower bodies. I placed my hands behind, holding my weakened frame, and looked up at the sky, trying to slow my breathing to a steady pace. Looking over at Victoria, I smiled as she reached into the water, picking up rocks and throwing them further into the river. Victoria must have sensed my eyes staring. She looked up, out of breath, and gave a smile, which curved up toward the left ear, forming cute dimples.

I am not sure what came over her, but she leaned forward. The event went in slow motion because every second her actions were reevaluated, but she continued to move slower toward my lips. As if my mind stopped working and I felt weak, I couldn't ponder how to escape the impending embarrassment. Victoria's soft lips landed on my lips, as my eyes widened, but hers remained closed. The kiss lasted a few seconds, but the shock at the gesture lasted longer, but I was glad that it happened. Victoria went back to thinking and lowered her head. Words couldn't be expressed, but the heart fluttered. The unexpected and surreal turn of events allowed me to escape into various thoughts and emotions.

In my head, I was jumping, screaming, and punching fists to the sky. My mind was racing, and entire body was numb with delight and surprised that a girl kissed me, and I couldn't have been happier. These were new emotions but felt exciting, as I wanted to share another kiss and experience the lips again.

I noticed the sun setting off in the distance. Remembering home and wondering the time, I looked at my watch and realized that time had gone.

"Oh crap, I have to get home. My parents don't know that we snuck outside," I said, anxious to leave, barely able speak.

I jumped up, ran, and slipped on my sandals that I placed near the trail. Victoria followed, and we raced up the long hill, back to the village; and once arriving at home, we split directions.

Once reaching the house, I opened the door, praying that my father wasn't home. As the door opened further, I saw Mom and Dad sitting on the couch, waiting. I tried to understand the expressions engraved on their faces, and it wasn't good.

My chin lowered as I took one step after another toward the couch. The sweaty hands soon crossed in front, trying to make myself small, showing the weaknesses and shame. My knees shook, my stomach ached, and my throat felt thick.

"Where have you been?" Dad said in a stern voice yet not shouting.

The question was met by silence as my body throbbed.

"Your father asked a question!" Mom shouted.

"By the river."

"Did we not tell you that you weren't allowed to leave the house unless we went?" Dad said.

"Yes!"

"This behavior scared us, and we cannot have you walking all over the place with the rebel group scoping out this village."

"Yes, Mom."

Mom's foot tapped on the ground with her ankles crossed, her hands folded back straight, and eyes locked on her target. Dad's hands tapped his knees as his feet raised. The dominating presence took over as he stood to his feet and now ascended over my scared body. I couldn't come to grips to look into his eyes as this might be met with deep sadness and stern expression.

Dad had enough of this and soon walked over, with his polished dress shoes tapping the concrete, as time appeared to stand still. He grabbed my shoulders, with enormous power and shook me back and forth. My head flung as he pushed harder. I wanted to say something, scream, and fight back; but instead, I took the abuse. The right hand raised high into the air and slapped my cheek. The sound of skin on skin echoed in the house, and tears welled up in my eyes. I grabbed my cheek, rubbing hard, as my eyes lowered.

"Do you understand? Do as you are told," Dad said.

I managed to mutter, "Yes, sir."

"Good. Then go to your room," Mom said in a comforting voice.

I ran to the room, and once there, my tears exited. For whatever reason, I did not want to cry in front of my father. He needed to see that I was a man and could take the punishment. Once in the room, I curled up in the corner with my legs pressed to my chest and let out more tears in the darkness. I didn't want to make noise because they could hear the echoes in such a small home. The rest of the night, I sat, not ready to make an appearance.

CHAPTER 7

There was a strange delight in me as I woke up early in the morning. Today was the first day of school, and it wasn't a normal feeling of returning from a long break and anxious to see friends. Today, I felt a fresh beginning, with new teachers, friends, and an education in a new language that hadn't become ingrained into my daily routines of village life. Many days, I was excited to go to school; and others, I wished I could curl up and die. Today was one of those times that I wanted to look my best to make a strong impression on the other students and teachers. Therefore, when I awoke from my restless sleep, I felt ready to start moving and walk a short distance toward the first day of the rest of my life and a chance to change my persona.

Dulce prepared the breakfast before I even exited my room. Most mornings, I had fried eggs, bread, and potatoes. This morning, I found a small salad with oil and vinaigrette dressing in addition to the usual breakfast. Not prepared to waste time, I made a sandwich with the eggs, bread, potatoes, and salad, and devoured the meal, getting up the second it was finished, forgetting to clear my plate.

Victoria mentioned that if you were late, the headmaster would whack your backside with a large stick that he finds every morning on the nearby tree. This notion forced my face to cringe in fear. The image of being late and bent over to receive an incomprehensible punishment couldn't happen on my first day of school, and so this image put a small fire in my step as I rushed through my morning routine.

Once breakfast finished, I went into my bedroom and grabbed the school uniform that my mother had bought. I laid the short-sleeved buttoned blue-collared dress shirt on the bed and went back to the makeshift closet that was made after the first week in our new home. The closet was a metal rod drilled into the corner of the room. This stretched three feet and had no doors to hide the contents. I grabbed a silver-colored pair of dress pants, placed those on top of the shirt, and then reached for the belt, which I kept in one of the suitcases under the bed. Right beside the suitcase, a buffed pair of black dress shoes sat, and tucked inside was a pair of silver dress socks.

Once I had the garments spread out in front of me, I undressed until I stood in my boxer shorts. Grabbing one garment after the other, I started to dress in the uniform until the last shoelace tied. Approaching a long mirror placed on the door, I examined my reflection. A slight smile broke free at the sight of the school uniform because I had never woken up in the morning and dressed so prim and proper, trying to get ready for school.

I brushed my teeth, grabbed a new basic black bag, and then Mom and I left the house. Mom didn't want to allow me to walk to school by myself, so she said that until her nerves ended, we would walk together. On the way to school, we stopped by Victoria's home, where she sat in front, waiting for our arrival. Her house looked similar to mine, except her home had a few flowers, which surrounded the front of the house and curved toward the back.

Victoria's uniform was the same colors, except for a knee-length skirt with knee-high socks.

She stood and walked toward us with her school bag strapped to one shoulder. Her mom, a young woman who wore an infectious smile, stepped out of the front door with a rag in her hand and waved good-bye. The three of us waved in unison and then turned away, heading toward school.

Once we arrived at the school, the headmaster stood at the gate with an improvised cane. Standing with his back as straight as a board, without an expression on his face that showed any kindness, as he continued to hit his hand with the cane. Children approached and greeted the towering man, but he said nothing or returned any reciprocal greeting of a nod, wave, or smile. The headmaster kept glancing at his watch, eager for time to start so that he could begin to whack the children. It felt strange that a man gained such pleasure out of causing such pain.

Victoria and I left my mom and approached the front gate.

Once we arrived at the headmaster, Victoria grabbed the sides of her skirt and curtsied with her head lowered to the ground out of respect. I wasn't sure what to do, so I bowed in front of him. Noticing my awkward bow, he couldn't help but smile. This must have been the first and last smile that I generated from this man.

Victoria and I entered the school, which wasn't much. To the right, a long stretch of classes, one after the other, with the first room being the offices, and the rest the lower school, grades one to three. To the left, across from the office, a long L-shaped building stood erected, which had one classroom after another. Each room had a large window, broken into twelve square panes. Each had several panes broken and now carried sharp, jagged edges. Many classrooms had doors while others had none.

Victoria led me around the L-shaped building to the second to the last classroom. Walking in, we saw a large blackboard in front of the student's desks. The teacher's desk was to the right of the blackboard and looked thirty years old. The chair was missing a wheel, and the cushion had a tear through the middle, exposing the foam. Taking a glance around the room, I saw nothing but dirty and blank walls. No student work, diagrams, or pictures brightened the room. The bland classroom demoralized children and crushed my spirit to learn. The floor covered with dirt, and the smell of chalk lingered in the air, which made it hard to breathe.

Students didn't sit in solitary desks. There were three rows of desks, and each was a long skinny table with a narrow bench that attached, which sat three to four students.

Many other students had taken a seat, chatting with friends. Victoria and I sat in the front row. The desks were so small I couldn't fit in them, and that was before the school bag was slid under my feet. The school bag was filled to the brim with writing pads and books that were purchased in Maxixe. The school bag made my feet ache, as there was no room to stretch. This was easier for Victoria because she was smaller than I was and could fit in the seat.

More students trickled into the classroom. Many didn't wear uniforms while others did. Many hadn't purchased the textbooks, which the school asked them to, while others had. I asked Victoria why students showed up to the first day of school unprepared, and her response was that they couldn't afford these things and thus shared textbooks. These same children walked into the classroom with torn shirts and jeans that appeared dirty with stains even after their mom washed them. These students appeared in sandals with disheveled toenails and dirty feet.

Looking around at other students, I noticed that those wearing the uniforms had buttons missing and torn pants at the side. One child had such a tear on the side that his skin just below his buttocks was exposed for everyone to see, and no one bothered to laugh or point. Other students had pants that were several years old and ended just above their ankles. Smaller children couldn't find pants small enough, so they had pants that were several sizes too large. Suddenly, I felt overdressed, looking at the rest of the classmates.

The classroom filled up, and students soon occupied each seat. The class waited for the teacher to come in, yet more students came strolling into the room, clapping their friends' hands. There were enough seats for twenty-five; and we now had thirty, then thirty-five, and finally forty students. Each small bench sat five, and a few sat six students. Four other students shared my bench. The students were so squished that it was hard to move my hand. Fortunately, I sat on the end, where I had the pleasure to write with my right hand. I couldn't imagine how Victoria was going to write.

Several more minutes passed, squirming in my seat with my writing pad and pen sitting in front, blank, but ready to be used. The teacher walked into the classroom. Students stood on their feet as she approached the middle of the room. She had a large stick in her hand and tapped it on the cement flooring.

"Good morning, class," she said in a stern voice, not wanting to give away any sense of friendliness.

"Good morning, Professor Mercia," the class recited in unison at their new teacher.

Professor Mercia looked as if she could be a lively and vivacious woman but wore herself in a dark and domineering manner. The nostrils snarled while her face bunched close together. She had fat cheeks and hair tied in a bun. Professor Mercia stood without an inch of skin exposed except her hands, which gripped onto her cane tight, exposing the small veins in her hand.

The class was instructed to take a seat, which we obliged. As she wrote the lesson that we started with on the board, three more young men appeared in front of the door. The children stopped, waiting to get permission to enter. The last young man to enter grabbed his backside and mimicked himself, yelling and saying "ahhhh" at being hit from the cane. The boy did this with a large smile, eyes squinted; and his face turned up toward the ceiling, trying to get a reaction from his audience. This drew a large laughter from the other students, which forced the reaction of the teacher. She turned around and gave an intense glare, pounding her desk with the stick until she achieved silence once more. The professor proceeded to scold the class and then continued to write on the board.

The rest of the morning was uneventful. We first completed math and then science. The teacher taught both subjects in Portuguese, which brought a revelation to an unknown fact that I understood most of what she was saying and conversed relatively well. After several weeks of language immersion, I was able to speak with some ease. The class then had a break, which most of the school just hung around and talked to each other. After break, a whistle blew, and everyone rushed off to class. We then had a history lesson; and just before lunch break, we had English, a topic that I enjoyed!

The teacher spoke little English. The professor started by copying a few sentences out of the book with a blank in place of several words. We needed to fill in the gap, which was easy. Near the end of the session, we started to work on how to greet people. My eyes rolled at how simplistic the lesson was, which achieved little stimulation from a native speaker. I wanted the nun to come and begin teaching, as she might be more advanced.

"You say, 'Good morn. How are you?' The response is 'Fine and you?'"

I was puzzled at the wording and use of the language. The whole lesson had perplexed me, and I couldn't take it anymore. I raised my hand, and she stopped talking and gave me a look as if I had done something wrong. As she realized that my hand wasn't going to retreat, she called upon me. "I think you might be wrong," I stated in the most polite way that I could find.

Victoria grabbed my knee and squeezed, trying to tell me that what I did was not something the teacher appreciated.

I continued saying, "I think you mean good morn-ING," pronouncing the *i-n-g*. "How are you? Then the response is 'I am fine, and how are you?'" Victoria slapped my knee, realizing that grabbing it did not get my attention. This particular teacher did not wish to be corrected by other students in a public manner, which I did.

The professor folded her arms and glared at me before breaking the long silence by stating, "Class, you are dismissed, except for . . ." and pointed at me, with the stick waiting for me to present my name. The long stick pointing toward my face forced a lump to form in my throat, and I appeared to have lost my words.

"Name," she yelled.

"Aderito," I stammered.

"Yes, you may stay."

The class got up and hurried out of the room. Most of the children, however, continued to watch from the door and apertures.

"Never correct me in public."

"Sorry, madam."

"Stand when I am speaking to you," she shouted it my direction. "Now come here." She gestured at me with her long finger. The finger and the sight of the stick made her look as if she meant to terrorize me and send shivers of fear through my spines. It worked! "You kids leave, right now," she yelled at the children who peeked through open door.

The children scurried away but returned just as quick when the teachers turned her back.

"Place your hands on the desk and stick your butt in the air," she said in Portuguese, pointing to the desk with her long stick.

"Are you serious?" I said, shocked at the thought.

"Do you think that I care that you are from America or who your mother and father are? You are in my class, and you will be punished the same as other students," she yelled, angry with my resistance to do what she was asking.

Walking over to the desk, I tried to slow down my steps, but I wasn't sure why because I just prolonged the pain and humiliation. Other children snickered from the doorframe and window as I almost cried before the pain of the cane came down my backside. My stomach turned, and my arms shook as I stared at the cane for the longest time.

Before she expressed the penalty, I had looked at the cane as an intimidating tool—but nothing more. Now the instrument that caused pain was a device that I came to dread. Approaching the desk, I placed my hands on the dirty surface and stepped backward as to lift my buttocks, as she directed.

Professor Mercia placed herself at the perfect place so that she could swing with maximum force. The cane swung back, and I could hear the whipping motion in the air, then a short silence, before a powerful whizzing sound echoed through the breeze, and then *whack*—the cane struck for the first time. I clenched my teeth together, moved my buttocks around, and jumped from the intense affliction. I had forgotten about the eyes that glued toward the scene until a loud giggle came from several of the children.

Another whack landed, this one harder than the first, and I clenched my fist tight and pounded the desk. In total, six strokes of the cane landed on my backside, each one more intense than the last, and each one drew more tears to well up in my eyes until they spilled over, landing on the desk. Once finished, I wiped my eyes of the tears before I turned toward the students. Once I turned, the students ran in every direction, trying not to be spotted. Walking out the front door, I looked off into the distance where Victoria leaned up against the tree.

I walked toward her and gave a weak smile as she rubbed my shoulder and whispered sorry into my ear. Off in the distance, a single building sat erected, and I left Victoria behind and headed toward the bathroom where I could assess the damages.

Once I entered the building, a strong smell of two hundred kids going to the bathroom for the last ten years hit me. The bathroom, by outside appearances, had not been cleaned. There was a large slab of concrete, which stretched the entire width of the building. This was a space for you to urinate. The urine drained itself outside through various drain holes drilled in the wall. Several small rooms had deep holes in the ground but had no doors to the latrines, so anyone walking in could see you going to the bathroom. I walked toward the opened latrines and saw a young boy who squatted in one, depositing his fecal matter. Saying nothing, I tried not to look, but it was impossible. The boy didn't appear to be bothered by my presence.

I walked into the latrine next to the younger boy. A cockroach spilled out from the deep hole, and flies swarmed around the blotches of young boy's feces, which had missed the toilet. The stench was overpowering, and it forced me to cover my nose with my one hand. I lowered my pants and underwear just enough so that I could get a peek at my bare skin but not enough to expose my entire backside for those who may enter. It was dark, but I managed to find light that shone into the room through a small crack in the wall. Six bright white streaks ran across my buttocks. My head lowered as I touched the tender flesh and winced at the pain that persisted.

A whistle blew off in the distance, which was the signal for me to go back to class. I rolled my eyes, because my lunch would sit untouched, and pulled up my pants, buttoned them, and made sure my shirt tucked into my pants. Feeling the time pass by, I raced out of the bathroom, through the field, and into the room, beating the professor.

Thirty minutes were spent waiting in the room before the teacher showed up halfway through the next class. Many times, I tried to eat lunch, but Victoria stopped me because the teacher might take the cane to my backside if she caught me with food inside the classroom. I kept explaining that she was late, but Victoria assured me that it didn't matter. Even though my stomach was aching from hunger, I decided to listen to her, because one beating with the cane was enough.

CHAPTER 8

I sat on the floor in the doorframe of my bedroom, peeking out from behind. At the end of the short corridor into the living room, my mother and father sat with a small group of people who were busy eating the snacks that Dulce had prepared. The men sat in the dim room, with the curtains drawn to block out the evening light. The day's events were the current topics that occupied the conversation, which was pointless. Even though the complications of the conversation wielded no interested, I sat in my pajamas, curious as to why the strangers gathered for what appeared to be a secretive meeting.

Mom and Dad were never successful at inviting people over to the house for social events. Socializing with others was an option but never at their home. They never liked the work that went into preparing the food and drinks for the people. Of course, I always sensed that this unsociable behavior spawned from my father's wish to occupy his time and thoughts within his introverted actions.

"Okay, can I have your attention?" my father said, trying to stop the constant chatter.

I sat up taller and placed my ear closer to the voices. There was a curiosity and mischievousness to my actions. I didn't know if eavesdropping on the meeting was wrong, but I knew my father wouldn't appreciate this behavior. But the thought of going to bed before knowing the contents of the agenda and the outcome of the decisions was forcing me to risk the punishment to gain knowledge that might affect my life.

"Well, I didn't invite you here to eat my food." The group laughed as my father made a rare attempt at humor. "A discussion needs to take place about RENAMO, who are terrorizing the children in the village."

"Yes, but what are we going to do?" the reverend stated. "The village is powerless to their guns and weapons."

"Can we get the FRELIMO army here to help protect the town?" Mom said off in the distance from the kitchen table, hidden from the wall.

"The FRELIMO soldiers come, but they only have the capacity to protect the large cities. They never come and protect these places. Plus, they are as bad as the RENAMO regime," an older man sitting in the far corner of the room on a plastic chair said in a cynical voice.

"So what do we do?" Dad said in an orotund voice.

"Nothing," another man said.

"And we do anything, we risk being shot, killed, or limbs cut."

"If we do nothing, then our children could be killed, kidnapped, or limbs cut off," my father said, leaning forward and pounding his knee with his fist, frightful and agitated by the lack of commitment.

"Listen, this is a very small town. The church sits at the beginning of the town. Could we not at least have someone look out for trucks and send a signal to the rest of the town to make sure that people are in their homes when they arrive?" the reverend said.

"That is a start," my father said. "Anything else we can do? Can we get guns? Can we protect our town with these guns?"

"That is a stupid idea. We will create a bloodbath of people and will lose. RENAMO's too strong, with too many people, and they will wipe out our town," the man in the corner said.

There was a long awkward silence as the men looked around the room, waiting for the next idea.

"So is there nothing else we can do?" my father said. "We will allow RENAMO to terrorize our women and children?"

"No . . . we will survive," the reverend stated.

"Listen, we don't want them to do this, but there is nothing we can do except get into the houses and stay out of sight."

"Then we have nothing else to discuss," my father said, lowering his head, shaking, and sighing under his breath.

I felt relieved that they said a fight should not come because the thought of my father with a gun fighting off RENAMO scared me. The men sat there in a long bout of silence before one got up and shook my father's hand and then exited out the door. One by one, the rest of the men showed their respect by taking his hand and exited until the reverend stood and shook his hand, wished him well, and left the house, closing the door.

Dad sat on his plastic chair for several minutes. Only half of him was illuminated because the other half hid behind the wall. The dim light above left him sitting there in a subtle glow, lighting up his body as if he were an angel. His body slouched forward, and both his elbows rested on his knees, with his hands placed on his head. Dad shook his head back and forth and at the same time caressed his forehead with both his thumbs.

Mom walked over to him and rubbed his back. The thought of her standing there, comforting him in a stressful time, was enough to guarantee him the little solace that he needed.

"Was this the right thing to do? Was it right to take Aderito to this place?" Dad said in a low whisper.

"I think you followed your heart," my mom said.

I knew she didn't mean those words, because multiple times, she expressed her disappointment; but she said those words knowing that if she didn't, it could wield no positive outcome.

Mom stood while Dad sat for the next half an hour, sitting in silence and listening to the charming sounds of crickets singing. I sat at the doorframe, staring at them. I enjoyed watching them comfort each other because I hadn't seen this in a long time. The two had been drifting apart ever since we moved to Mozambique, but now stood united.

As they stood there, my eyes began to get tired. I closed them for a brief second and then opened them to see them still standing beside each other, oblivious as to where I was. My eyes closed once more, then my body went limp, and my head slid to the ground, with my hands tucked under, acting as a pillow. My feet curled to my chest, and then I slid into a deep sleep, next to the doorframe on the freezing cement floor.

PART 3

Renamo

CHAPTER 9

We had been in Mozambique for several months. I now spoke Portuguese as good as the rest of the children.

Permission was granted to spend our days by the river. My mother convinced that the shelter and the hidden secrecy by the woods and deep bank provided more protection from the enemies than the small home. The security and peacefulness of the river also shielded the innocent eyes from the atrocities that were starting to become standard.

Victoria and I spent most of Saturdays alone, except for the occasional woman coming with her dirty clothes propped on her head in a wicker basket while her children were ready to bathe. We always tried to stay away from the women working on Saturdays. I didn't want to run and play in the river while children were bathing next to me, so we went further upstream and had fun running, jumping, and splashing.

The day's events—full of play, laughter, and tranquility—were coming to an end as the sun was setting and the air was becoming colder. Enjoying the company, we sat as long as possible. The night came closer, and there was no hope to prolong the day by another second, so reluctantly, we walked toward the narrowed trail and toward the village.

When we arrived at the top of the hill, Victoria noticed men with guns and the vehicle that we dreaded parked near the town center. Victoria grabbed my hand and pulled me to the ground until my face absorbed into the dead grass, and we crawled over to a large shrub that we thought was protection.

I peeked through a small hole, where a tall man with thick boots appeared with an AK-47 and green army clothes that covered his body and grabbed a young boy whom I remembered from school. The boy was screaming, yanking, and tugging his small body; but he was no match for the dominating man that stood over him. The parents of the boy ran toward the truck, trying to stop the imposing man; but the mother met the butt of the gun to her face, knocking her to the ground. The father was shot in front of the child, who let out a deafening cry before he was thrown headfirst into the pickup truck. Two men in the back of the truck pointed their guns an inch away from the young boy's head, daring him to run, and if he did, those would be the final steps. The boy succumbed to his fate, lowered his head, and accepted that he would be taken. He stopped crying and showed his captors that he was strong and could take any abuse that they inflicted.

Men, women, and children ran through the village, trying to get to safety. The RENAMO men shot rounds of their ammunition in the air and turned the weapons on the innocent civilians, who screamed, ran, and fell to their deaths. Scanning the village, I tried to find my parents, but they weren't visible. I hoped that they were safe in their homes and then saddened to think that they were worried.

"What will they do with him?" I panted, feeling my heart pound. My eyes continued to scan back and forth, as sweat dripped from my head. My lungs came in and out, and I felt like I had just run a marathon, but I didn't—I was petrified.

"Make him a soldier," Victoria stated.

The RENAMO army patrolled the village for a few minutes, and then two more boys found themselves hauled into the truck. The only appearing emotion was fear, running, crying, and boys being beaten and soon captured by feared moguls.

As we lay, trembling in the tall dead grass, a footstep crept closer. I didn't want to look. Lying with my head lowered, I hoped the impression was off in the distance and prayed that whoever this person was, he came in peace.

Someone was staring at me, so I closed my eyes, hoping that the elongated stare went away. Without notice, a sharp kick dug in my side. The sharp pain intensified as a large boot hit my rib with extreme force. I curled my body and gasped for air. I panted, and just when the pain dispersed, a second blow to the same spot landed even harder on my rib cage. Choking for a single breath, I was unable to make a sound. As I lay there, panting, I heard Victoria let out a loud scream as the man hoisted her to her feet. The man gave a hard slap to her face as she fell back to her knees, weeping as she rubbed the stinging tender flesh.

I turned around and lay on my back, looking up at a shadowy figure. He appeared to be tall, mean, and brutish. The man leaned forward until his face lit up by the setting sun. The same person who saw us in the bushes that one day appeared again. The scar on his face stretched from his eye to his ear. His teeth were stained yellow and gave off an aroma of a dead man. The logical explanation was because he had been lost inside for so long, and the youthful image had stopped trying to escape and was now dead.

Fear quaked throughout my body. The sight of him standing, with a snarled lip showing half his teeth, forced me to release urine. The urine trickled around my body, landing on my backside. He grabbed me by the shirt and hoisted me to my feet. The urine began to trickle out of my shorts and landed on his boot. Noticing the watery substance continuing to flow toward his boot, he let go, allowing me to crumble to my knees, and then shook his boot, trying to get it dry. The same boot, now covered in urine, kicked my face hard. Blood started to come from my mouth. I wanted to cry, but a weep was the only sound that came. Victoria lay beside me—crying, trying to say something—but nothing came out.

The man took his heavy boot and placed it on my mouth. I closed my lips as he pressed his boot harder and harder, digging my upper lip into my teeth, tearing the gums, and releasing blood. The boot pried open my mouth and went inside, forcing my mouth to open wide, hurting my jaws and teeth as the flesh tore open. "Taste the urine because that may be all you get for food today."

The man took the boot out of my mouth and watched for a second as I tried to collect myself. "Lick it. Clean my boot, you scum," he shouted.

I paused, not knowing what to do; but out of fear, I opened my mouth, stuck out my tongue, and reached out toward the urine. Once I was a few inches away, he took the end of his gun and hit me hard on my backside. "Lick it," he demanded. I began to lick the salty substance off his boot. However, my obedience did not please the man as the end of his gun kept landing on my back. I licked faster and harder until the only thing left was my saliva.

I tried to spit out the urine, but it was useless. I lay crying, gasping for air, and trying to come up with any plan that might help.

The zipper of his pants moved downward. Victoria looked up and said nothing but mimicked a no. I looked around and saw the man pull out his penis. Victoria was kicked toward me, so we now sat close to each other, weakened and propped up by the bushes. He began to urinate on the two of us as we moved from side to side but didn't dare run. I tried to keep my mouth closed, but it was impossible. The man urinated on our faces, and the watery substance entered our mouths and trickled to our bodies as if it were a waterfall. The taste was overpowering. Victoria found the tears and began to cry. Her body shook, trying to avoid the urine. Once the man had finished, he glared at me in a strange satisfaction. The man erected the gun and ordered us to get up from where we sat.

Victoria and I hesitated, but lifted our bruised and beaten bodies to a standing position. "Walk," he demanded.

We walked toward the truck, which was a few hundred feet away. I felt as if I were walking toward an executioner and that at the end of the walkway assorted posts lined the truck. The soldiers would tie us, and then we would wait to be executed in front of the village. However, my ending wasn't quick or painless; instead, we walked toward the truck and got in where there were various other boys sitting. Scared at what might happen next, Victoria continued to shake and scream at the fate that had gripped us. I wanted to cry, but I felt inclined to be strong.

The car started to move. We passed close by my home, and I looked for my parents so they knew where I was and could fight for my release. My mom, who looked out the window, glanced at me sitting in the back of the truck. She flung the door open and ran out in her bare feet. The car took a U-turn to start heading out of the village.

My mom was screaming and chasing after the truck. She was crying and flailing her arms. "Stop . . . you bastards have my baby," she screamed in her best Portuguese.

I fixated my eyes on her but didn't stretch my arms out because I tried not to show any emotion, for her sake, but I couldn't resist. A single tear rolled through my urine-soaked body. Mom reached her arms out and continued to run through town, screaming at the onlookers, who did nothing.

The truck sped up, leaving a large cloud of dust, which splattered into my mom's face. Her image disappeared, and my soul went dead. Once the dust had cleared and the truck started to ascend the hill, I caught a glimpse of a woman running, knowing it must have been her, continuing the pursuit. The truck continued, and soon, my mom had disappeared from my sight. I knew that she was continuing to run and continued this until the energy escaped, and she fell silent on the street to weep and pray.

Was this going to be the last time I gazed at her? Was this going to be the end? Where were they taking me? Questions raced through my mind, but I had no answer for the endless stream of queries. Victoria placed her hand on my knee and squeezed, but I didn't smile, as was my normal reaction, because not a single glimmer of hope found a way into my emotions. This felt as if it were the end.

***

The trip lasted several hours until the truck pulled into a large compound where more men walked aimlessly in an effort to show that they were doing something productive toward the cause. The truck stopped, and the kids were ushered out. The man with the scar grabbed Victoria and me by the shirt and pulled us behind a large building where cement cracked and fell, creating small piles of rubble.

"Get undressed . . . NOW," he screamed.

Victoria and I undressed and threw our clothes off to the side. We felt exposed and vulnerable, positioned in the alley. As I looked over at Victoria, she covered her breasts with one hand, and a dark silhouetted body trembled; and as her eyes grazed the ground, small subtle weeping sounds exited her mouth. The darkened sky provided no hope as I wondered what my mother and father were doing. Pictures of their somber tears, as the reverend comforted them, brought comfort, and I hoped that they looked up to the same stars and that we experienced the same moment.

The man walked away and returned a few minutes later, holding a hose that he had crimped to avoid water rushing out. He moved his gun to be positioned behind his back and let out the crimp, allowing water to flow. The man placed his thumb in the end to offer more pressure and then pointed the hose toward us, as the water doused our bodies.

The water was freezing. Victoria and I lowered our bodies to the ground and shivered as the man rushed water on our bodies to try to rinse off the urine. He did this for several minutes until he threw the hose to the side and walked away, leaving us trembling in the forming mud at our feet. Water dripped from our opened mouths, gasping for a single ray of hope. Victoria and I stood up, and soon, he arrived back with new clothes.

A tattered unadorned white T-shirt and a torn blue pants were given to me while Victoria placed her shirt and shorts over the bruised and battered body. The man then directed us to walk in front, as he held the gun to our backs. We walked out of the alley and through a long stretch of buildings. Near the end of this stretch was a large structure that had four walls and no individual rooms. Walking in, we saw children lying on the floor. The stench of the unbathed kids hit me hard as my nose moved from side to side, trying to avoid the smell. They had fear on their faces and not a single smile among them. The children's youthfulness had finished, and their ardor and spirit were dead.

"This is where you will sleep. Tomorrow, we start training. Come with me." He pointed at Victoria in a low creepy voice.

I reached my hand out, but she was led out the door before our hands could touch. Three guards stepped in front of the doorway to make sure no one left. I walked over to a small window with several steel bars bolted to the concrete. I watched as the man led Victoria over to a small room across from where we were staying. As he opened the door, a raggedy dirty bed sat lying in the center of the room. The light was turned on, and Victoria was pushed into the room, landing hard on the thin springy bed. The door closed, but a small crack allowed me to see what he was doing and to fuel my anger.

Reaching toward Victoria, he grabbed the ratty, torn shirt and tried to lift it up and over her body. She resisted and pulled away, but he reacted and landed multiple hard blows toward her face. The screams pierced through the walls, which proved to be pointless as no one came to her rescue.

Victoria lay on the bed as her chest was rising and falling. She was in danger, which was clear from her reaction, and I wished that it ended. The man grabbed the shirt and pulled it off, followed by the shorts and underwear until she was feeble. I heard her wail and then reach toward him, trying to make it stop, but he struck her face and continued. Victoria said nothing and did nothing but lay insensibly, waiting for the rape to stop.

It lasted five minutes, but in those five minutes, she became a broken woman. He stopped and waited for her to dress. Once they left the building, I ran back to the front door and waited for her to enter. The door creaked open, and he shoved her inside as I stared into her eyes, trying not to look at the bruises and the blood that dripped from the side of her mouth. Victoria opened her mouth and let out a whisper of a scream. Victoria's teeth painted red, and her lips quivered. I looked deep into her eyes and saw fear. The only thing that I could think of was to give her a long hug and walk her over to the corner of the building near the front door. I didn't dare let go of her, as I knew she needed this, and if we were going to survive or escape, we needed each other.

Victoria and I lowered to the ground until we both sat. The embrace of her shivering body felt warm. She cried into my shoulder, leaving bloodstains on the dirty shirt. Victoria cried herself to sleep, with her head resting on my lap. Placing one hand on her shoulder, I grabbed the bottom of my shirt and wiped away the blood that I could see and the tears that still lingered around her eye.

I rested my head on the cement wall and caressed her shoulder, closing my eyes and falling asleep.

CHAPTER 10

Several weeks or months passed, and we were held in the small room, unable to leave. The only source of light was a small window, which the children gathered in front of, trying to see what was happening. The only time an adult came into the room was to spread the message of the rebel army, trying to brainwash the children. They only let out to be hosed off, relieving us of our stench, and then rushed back into the small room to wait for the morning to come.

The door flew open, which made a loud thumping sound as it slammed toward the wall. A man different from any of the others I had seen entered, dangling a cigarette out of his mouth. The young man waved his gun in the air and yelled, "Get up. Line up outside the building," he said, pointing his gun toward the exit.

The children had no feelings and no hope of our return, so we did so without resistance. The children lined up and stood, staring at the man. The man stared at us until another soldier came, holding a large pot of steaming food. With his free hand, he stirred the food with a large silver ladle.

"Hold out your hands," the man stated.

The children did as we were told. The heavyset man with a fat neck approached the children, stopped in front of each child in line, and placed one scoop of beans in our hands. I waited as he made his way in front of me. He plopped the beans into my hand, which were so hot that my hands burned, but I didn't dare drop them because this might be my only meal during the day. My head lowered, and I started to eat the food out of my hands as if I were less than human, as if I were a criminal or a pig eating out of the trough. Still, none of this mattered. I was so hungry that I devoured the beans, trying to be careful that few landed on the raised cement porch. Once the beans finished, I started to lick my fingers and in between, trying to get every ounce of the liquid into my belly.

Once finished, a man walked up to me, staring at my cleaned hands. "Still hungry?"

"Yee-sss," I stammered to an answer.

"Well, it looks like you have dropped some. Go ahead and eat that."

Looking at the rest of the children, I noticed that most of them, including Victoria, were on their knees, eating the leftover food. Dropping to my knees, I pondered how a dog eats as the man hovered, staring intently at my shaking body. I grabbed the food with my hands, and then I felt a sudden sharp kick to my sore side. "Eat them like the dog you are," he shouted.

I started to eat the beans with my mouth pressed to the porch before realizing that this was causing more work, so I stuck out my tongue, started to pick pieces of beans that now had dirt and mud covering the taste, and swallowed them whole.

I continued to do this until there wasn't a single drop on the porch, and then I stood back up as if I was a human being ready to take back my dignity. The children waited until the others had finished, and then the adults accompanied us away from the building. We passed the rest of the compound, which had scattered structures placed in no logical order. Near the end of the compound was a large field, and at the end of this field was a single brick wall.

A dominating man stood in front of the children with his hands behind his back. The man wore a large hat that had an eagle flying and military-style uniform that was solid blue and ironed straight. The uniform had medals and various stripes that decorated the high-powering military officer. He stood personable, tall, and confident as if he were a prominent figure within the compound. Next to him was the scar-faced man. Victoria and I didn't dare look into his face.

The commander looked at Victoria and said, "The girl will be a servant. She will not be fighting with the boys. Take her away and make her do womanly work."

A soldier whisked her away, which left me alone and exposed to handle these men and their strange, frightful tactics.

"My name is Commander, nothing else. You will call me Commander. This is my partner, Zélio. We are now your family, and you can forget the life you used to lead. You are now soldiers in the rebel movement, and your first task is to learn to be soldiers."

"Everyone on their feet," Zélio yelled.

We jumped to our feet and were quick to be handed a fake bayonet rifle. We stood with our backs slouched over and guns dangled to our sides. Zélio came around to each boy and yelled for him to straighten up and act as soldiers. Zélio stepped toward me and squinted his eyes as he pondered my stance and ability to behave like a soldier, as I looked more like a puppet.

"Stand up tall," he shouted at me as he stood a few feet away, spewing spit and his aroma into the air.

I paused for a second, but that was all the time he needed. Zélio punched me in the stomach and watched me hold it and breathe in and out, letting out a small scream. Zélio grabbed my chin, lifted me up, and then yelled at me to stand up straight. I did so with quick speed. I stood with my back straight and arms pressed to my side and my face looking forward. Zélio lifted the fake gun, which was dangling to the ground. He made my right hand hold the butt and my left hand hold the wooden barrel. Zélio then pressed the gun toward my chest, and I now looked like a soldier.

Zélio led the soldiers in a formation around the wall where several stuffed dummies made from scraps stood. The simple creations were a piece of wood dug into the ground and wrapped with foam. There were no hands to the dummies or feet. One after another, we bashed and thrust our makeshift weapons toward the fake humans as if they were alive. If we didn't do it hard enough, the training officers were quick to apply a swift punishment of several lashes to our backs with a long belt. I learned soon after the first two beatings that I needed to hit it hard enough to kill a man.

It was my third attempt, my eyes became darker, and a demon consumed my body. I ran up to the dummy and hit it hard with the butt of the gun and then let out a massive scream as I turned my gun around and stabbed the dummy hard in the gut. This was done with such a force that the wooden support beam broke near the bottom, and the dummy toppled to the ground, bouncing once before resting. Standing over the dummy, I let out one mighty scream as if I were a monstrous maniac ready for the kill. The surrounding instructors clapped as if I had just performed a miracle. I didn't hear their glorious yells as I was letting out my own. I think this was the first moment that I had, where I could scream and let out my wrath on something, and so I did.

Zélio walked over to me, rubbed my head, gave me a gentle tap on my back, and ushered me to the end of the line. I looked over at the commander, who was pleased with my aggression. This felt awkward, and I didn't know how to react, but maybe the way to react and please the controlling man and find a glimmer of hope to escape was to act as if I were proud.

The rest of the day, we performed war games. With each game, the anger boiled up into me until it toppled over, and I let out more anger and was ready to attack. I hated what I had become because I felt a wish to battle and to beat people. This wish to hurt someone was a new feeling in which I wasn't sure how to handle. I didn't know whom I wanted to hurt, but I wanted an avenue to let my anger flow. Maybe I wanted to kill the people who captured me or maybe to single my energy toward the commander, but at this point, I was happy to hurt anything.

Once the sun set, the adults led the group to an open space, with just a few hoses, where the boys were made to strip and shower in the open. The children and I stood on the dead grass, naked, hosing each other off and lathering ourselves with soap that we shared among each other. Once we finished, we put the clothes that we wore during the day back on and shivered our way back to our rooms.

Zélio told me to come with him.

The commander was sitting at the table with a plate of bread and a glass of wine. The commander stood up tall and waited for his guests to arrive. I was asked to accompany him, which was an honor that most soldiers relished. However, I didn't want this honor and wished that I could turn them down, but this sounded as if it were a demand and not a question.

"Have it. It's yours. You have earned it," he said, gesturing toward the bread and wine.

I didn't waste any time. I dug into the meal and drank the wine as if I were a dog and scared that this was a joke and the food would soon be whisked away, in an attempt at a mind game to control my behavior. The commander just smiled as he waited for me to finish.

"What you did today was impressive. I think you will be an outstanding fighter and will make me proud." There was a long pause as if I needed to answer to his compliment or acknowledge that it was given, but I wasn't sure what should be said; so I sat, slouched in the chair, scared to speak in front of him. The commander watched my eyes move back and forth, trying to find an exit, so he continued, "You know, I have something for you." He reached over, grabbed the base of my chair, and pulled it toward him. The commander reached for my hand, took out a large tan rubber tube, and tied it just above my elbow.

"This will help you forget about what happened yesterday."

My veins popped out as he reached into a bag that was placed by his feet and pulled out a long syringe. I flinched backward, and then he pulled my hand closer. The commander held it tight as he pushed the needle deep into my vein. He pressed the syringe, which released the substance into my bloodstream. Within a few seconds, I became relaxed, my body slouched further into the chair, and my head rested on the back. My eyes rolled upward, showing the whites, and I twitched several times as the substance took control of my body. The sensation filled my desire, my worries escaped my thoughts, and my mind and body felt free from any terrible thing that might have happened.

The commander released the rubber tube and watched me relax into the chair and fall asleep. The commander laughed and ordered his men to carry me back to the sleeping quarters.

Once there, Victoria saw me and tried to wake me. Victoria thought I was dead. I could hear her voice, shouting; yet my body was sedated into a deep trance, and I could not respond. Victoria rested her head on my body and lay awake, hearing my heart pound in a rapid beat.

CHAPTER 11

Two weeks passed. Every day, we woke up, ate our beans, and went to work. We played war games, and when we didn't do it right, we felt the pounding fists. The soldiers tore our spirits apart and built them back up with presents and surprises such as a good meal. I became reliant on the regime for my needs, even though what they provided was meager. I felt as if I belonged to them, and they needed me. If they asked, I couldn't deny their wishes, and I would carry out any illegal act. Once the day's chores finished, the commander rewarded the efforts with a hit of heroin. I craved this. I needed it. By day's end, I was so desperate for the sensation that I begged the commander, and he always obliged me with the request.

I saw Victoria less and less. Victoria always tried to tell me what had happened during the day, but that was often not possible with me being sedated with the magic drug and her being starved. Nearly every day, she was raped by a different man. This was becoming a normal thing, and it was rare that she resisted. Victoria became passive in her willingness to lie down and take the abuse and too tired to fight. Victoria tried to pull away from the men, who would land swift and violent slaps or pummels to the head. This, of course, led to fresh bruises around her otherwise soft face. The commander demanded that she serve him, treating her more like a dog and less than a servant. The commander never had intercourse with his animals, so he never touched her.

I wished that I could be near her and protect her, but I was too high. As a result, it was hard for me to understand what was happening or to see that she was in trouble. Victoria was becoming grotesquely gaunt, with her eyes drooped and her face and body painted with fresh and old bruises. Had I been more aware, someone might have died.

Every night a few guards carried me in the sleeping quarters because I couldn't walk on my own due to the sedation caused by the endless drugs that the compound provided. Victoria found herself on my bed, lying next to me with her head resting on my chest. Victoria enjoyed the rising and falling of my lungs and listening to the slow beat of my heart. I was never conscious enough to sense her resting on my body but found her in the morning, with her arms wrapped tight around my waist.

The next morning we rushed through breakfast, led out to a large field, and told to stand in front of the large cement wall. That particular morning, people treated me different. The soldiers greeted me with warmth instead of insults. The soldiers still forced me to eat breakfast like a dog, but I thought it was strange that instead of hitting me or yelling, they were gentle and kind.

The children stood at attention in front of the commander. I looked and acted as if I were a soldier, confident and ready for the brutal day's events. I waited with my back straight and my feet and arms together. My head was facing forward, and I showed little emotion. The commander directed us to sit, which the soldiers replied with a deafening "Yes, sir."

"One of you is ready to be a soldier," the commander bellowed.

Two men pulled out a man from behind the wall. The man struggled as they dragged him, kicking and screaming. The men kicked the traitor several times hard in the rib cage and told him to be quiet. Once in front of the soldiers, they kicked his knees hard from behind and made to kneel in front of the eager eyes. He was a skinny man, with a full beard. The bound hands were tied tight behind his back. He was sweating as he gazed at the young children, who looked as rugged as soldiers did yet innocent as children.

"Aderito has proven that he is a man and is ready to show us his loyalty."

I rose to my feet and stood next to the commander, who gave me a real hand pistol. I looked at this gun. For a brief second, I thought of turning the gun to the commander and then taking my own life. It was something that I thought, but after five days, I was grappling with the two families. I still remembered my father and mother, but the drugs and the beatings were slowing making them a distant recollection. The soldiers, who were a new and stronger family who took care of me, were the thoughts that lingered on my mind.

Walking toward the man, I held the gun toward his head and paused. My head raised as I looked toward the commander, who nodded, signaling for me to continue. I paused again before the commander said, "He was caught supporting FRELIMO, and he is a traitor to the movement and needs to be killed."

I looked at the man who shook his head and pleaded for me to show him mercy. However, at that moment, I believed in the commander's words and knew that this traitor and scumbag needed to die. The traitor had what was coming to him. My hands started to sweat, and my neck and back blanketed in my own perspiration. My eyes narrowed on the subject as I grabbed the trigger. Shaking back and forth, I took in deep breaths, trying to contemplate my actions.

Mixed with emotions, I felt the moral thing to do was to spare his life and give him back his democracy and freedom. However, the thing expected of me was to show my manhood and kill him for his sins. I couldn't contemplate right from wrong, and so I closed my eyes and pulled the trigger.

The sound of the bullet echoed around the land, lingered in the air for a long time, and could be heard for miles. When I opened my eyes, the man was lying at my feet; blood was spreading outward and heading toward the commander.

My stomach was weak, and my body stood at a standstill as I contemplated the sight of a man, who just a few seconds ago held his breath, praying for his fate, and now lay lifeless before my feet. Lifeless because of my finger and my brutal act of passage into manhood.

I was standing in shock as I had done it, killed a man, and now I was part of this movement. My emotions torn between the morals of childhood lessons and the evil that appeared. The devil inside said that this was the right thing to do while the nobility was telling me to run. The demon was taking over, and the voice inside my head teaching me right from wrong was getting quieter.

I didn't dare move away from the blood but allowed it to surround me, as I couldn't take my eyes off the man who now had a bullet that pierced through his head. The man's life had ended, and I wasn't sure why. All I knew was that my new father said it was the best thing to do, and he must have known what was best for the movement and my new brothers and sisters.

The commander gave me a machete. I looked at this weapon, pondering the careful deed. He took the gun from my hand and whispered in my ear, "Now cut his head off, like the animal he was."

I wasn't sure what to think. The man was dead, but to make sure that the punishment was swift, I needed to take his head. Was this a ritual within the compound? Was releasing his head going to allow his soul to enter the depths of hell where it belonged? I became confused and didn't know why my father asked me to do such a thing. There was a clear idea to defy him, but the wish to be a good son dictated the actions I took on that day.

I raised the machete into the air and reviewed the decision that was inevitable, and I let the rage enter my body and then struck hard on the neck of the bloodied man. Blood spurted out, spraying my face. I kneeled in the blood that covered the concrete. I looked over at my comrades who wore the same shocked face. My chest allowed air in and out, with my eyes squinted, mouth opened wide, and eyebrows lowered. The crowd, for a brief second, saw the devil. I raised the machete into the air, let out a loud-piercing scream, and then began to hit the neck repeatedly. Each time, more flesh was cut, bones crushed; and as a large blade cut through the last piece of skin, the head broke free from his shoulders and rolled away from where I kneeled. My hands, arms, legs, and head covered with blots of blood. Red strokes and streams ran through my clothes. I knew the moral thing to do was to cry, but that showed weakness. Also, I knew that the innocent boy who came into the compound was now a man, and the man stood up tall and brave in the face of his family.

"Raise the head up. Show the children how you became a man today," the commander said.

I threw the machete to the ground, listening to the hushed clanking sound of the weapon hit the blood next to the headless man. I grabbed the head with both hands and held it over mine. Blood dripped from the veins and splatted on my head, yet I didn't care. A strange satisfaction overcame me. I looked into the eyes of the other soldiers who cheered. I pumped the head into the air several more times, as if it were my first trophy, before dropping it to the ground, allowing it to roll away for several feet, finding a resting spot with his eyes looking up at me. Veins spewed out as I saw the neck bone, yet I was more concerned at the eyes that refused to close as if they were staring deep inside me.

"Today, we will cut up this body and feed you him for dinner. This will protect you from FRELIMO troops," the commander said to the crowd of young children. No one even questioned him. We agreed that this must be the best action, not because it was logical but because the commander had said it, and he must know what he was doing.

The rest of the children went on with their normal daily routine while I went back with the commander. I took a long shower to get the blood off and then was given a new change of clothes, which was the first time I had changed since I had been at the camp.

The commander showed me to my new room that had a small bed, which was a change that I welcomed; but at the same time, I was perturbed over Victoria and her safety without my protection and comfort.

That evening, the rest of the children sat outside the large dining patio while the official soldiers sat at the tables. Victoria arrived.

Victoria walked over to the table and gave me a slight smile, yet most of her attention was on the commander and Zélio, who sat across from me. Zélio put his hand around her and caressed her back. He then slid his hands under her shirt and rubbed her bare skin. The rage sat in my stomach as I could not raise my fist, shout, or cry at the sight of Victoria being caressed and broken.

"She is a pretty thing," the commander laughed as I nodded in agreement. "Would you like her?"

"All for myself?" I said, perking up at the thought.

I didn't perk up because I wanted to have sex. I thought that by making her mine, I could keep other men from raping her, and I could steal food to be given to her every night.

"All for yourself. You can do what you like to her."

"So no one else can touch her."

"If you would like, consider it a gift from me. You came here together, so I think it may be fitting that she becomes yours."

"Very much," I said.

The commander stood up and looked at the rest of the soldiers who were busy being served. "The young lady . . . Victoria is the newest soldier's girl, so you keep your hands off her unless . . . of course, you are given permission," he said, laughing, which reciprocated laughter from the rest of the men. The commander sat relaxed onto his chair. "Go get Aderito his meal and bring me my steak," the commander directed Victoria.

Victoria came back a few minutes later, bringing a bowl of stew, with a distinctive human flesh that was to be given to the child soldiers. Victoria gave the commander a plate with rice and a large steak dinner. I was given a bowl of soup. "Eat," he commanded to me. "Victoria, you may go, but tonight you must pleasure your friend." Victoria nodded and left the table.

I dipped my spoon into the bowl and stirred it around for a few minutes. Focusing on the chopped meat, I couldn't help but picture the young man's face in the soup. I knew that if I refused the meal, this might be a sign of weakness. If I ate the food, I could be sick with sadness and remorse for the actions and crimes that I committed. However, this remorsefulness would be masked with the belonging of the movement and need to obey the commander.

I grabbed my first spoonful of the thick stew and raised it toward my mouth. Steam lifted into my nose as I hesitated to enter this cannibalistic act. Everyone's eyes were on me, including those of the commander, who refused to eat until I started. There was a large cubed piece of cooked meat in the middle of a spoonful of stew. I opened wide; closed my eyes, placing the spoon into my mouth; and, with one motion, emptied it on to my tongue. I bit the meat as my eyes squinted upward, and my face bunched together. The meat was fatty, tender, and seasoned with a strong chicken stock. The thought that I had eaten human flesh made my stomach queasy, and my appearance of disgust showed for the adult soldiers to laugh. I continued chewing until the meat went into my stomach, and the next bite went in my mouth.

Out of an effort to finish the fleshy meal, I ate as quick as I could, because the longer I waited, the longer I might sit and squirm in my anguish. I told the commander that I needed to use the bathroom and asked to leave the table. The commander gave me permission, as I pushed away from the emptied bowl. I walked away from the table, and my stomach bounced and churned the food. My mind raced with the images of killing this man then devouring his flesh for a sick pleasure, and knew that a piece of his body now rested in my stomach. Once I knew I was away from the dinner crowd and could not be seen anymore, I ran across the compound and past my old room to the bathroom. The bathroom was a pit latrine, but I didn't care.

I flew to my knees and stuck my head near the opening where people went to the bathroom. My eyes fixated on the feces that were waiting to decompose. The smell was overpowering, which did nothing for my queasy stomach. I couldn't hold it anymore. The dinner, which I devoured a few minutes ago, came up and came with force. I could see the chunks of my victim escaping my mouth and into the deep well of shit. The vomit continued to pour, causing intense aching pains in my throat. Once the last watery vomit left my mouth, I spit several times into the latrine, trying to get every bit of the substance off my tongue and diminish the taste.

Just outside the latrine, there was a bucket of water to wash your hands. It wasn't the cleanest water, but it didn't matter. I bent over the bucket and began to splash water on my face. I grabbed a cupful in my hands and raised it to my lips where I sipped, trying to get the vomit from my mouth.

Deep hard breaths gave disturbing sounds in a silent night. Clearing my throat, wiping the sweat off my head, I strolled back to where the commander was sitting. Next to him was Victoria. The commander beckoned her to take me back to my room for "fun times," as he put it.

Victoria did as the commander demanded and grabbed my hand to go with me to my new bedroom. Once in there, I closed the door behind and looked outside, nervous that someone might follow. The commander stared at my room, with his head tilted to the side and his hands clasped together on his lap. His eyes squinted, and his body and face resonated with curiosity and skepticism as to the actions that I might take. Ignoring his presence, I sat on the bed.

"Why did you ask to take me?" she demanded an answer.

"Because then, I could try to make sure no one else harms you and maybe I could sneak food to you," I said, continuing to look through the casement to make sure no one was coming.

"Every time I see you, you look out of it. What are they giving you?"

"They keep sticking a needle into my arm, and it makes me real high. They didn't give it to me today, but I am craving it. It makes me feel good."

"You can't have that stuff. You will die in here if you keep taking it."

I looked once more out the window and saw the commander talking to a soldier and pointing toward my room. The soldier walked down the steps and toward my quarters. "Someone is coming," I stated in a panic.

I lay on top of her, just as the door opened. The man smiled as he saw us lying there together. I turned my head and yelled at him, "Don't you see, we are busy. Get out of here."

The man nodded and then closed the door. I lay there for a few minutes as I listened to his footsteps walk away back to the commander. Once I felt that it was safe, I got up from where I lay, and I was able to catch a glimpse of Victoria with her shirt pulled up, just below her breasts. Victoria was skin and bones. I knew she had lost weight from the low cheekbones that exposed from her hanging skin, but the sight of her stomach was unbearable.

"How often do you eat?"

"Whenever the commander can't finish his meal, he gives it to me."

"How often?" I demanded.

"A few scraps per day."

I shook my head. I looked back outside and noticed that the soldiers were busy playing cards and talking to themselves.

"Wait here. I think I can sneak to the back where the kitchen is and get you bread or something."

"Don't. It's too dangerous."

"It's also dangerous to not eat . . . Wait here."

I didn't wait for her to convince me otherwise as I rushed out the door and across the walkway. I hid behind the bushes, looking up on the patio where the rest of the soldiers sat. As I rushed, I saw a soldier off in the distance, patrolling the compound. My heart pounded as I hid behind a large bush until his back turned away from me and it was safe for my misguided heroism to continue. I turned around the corner and could see, off in the distance, the kitchen, which lay adjacent to the dinner patio. I took one more look around, and I couldn't see anyone.

The comfort of my hiding had gone as I rushed across the open field, exposing my thievery. Once there, I noticed several people cleaning. I took a deep breath and entered. "The commander wants a plate of bread to eat while he plays cards."

The kitchen staff didn't even bother to double-check the story or look at my eyes moving back and forth and my body swaying around, trying to hide the lie. They handed me bread, and I walked out of the kitchen. Once they weren't looking, I ran back across the small field and scooted back around the circled patio where the soldiers sat and then back to the room where Victoria waited.

Victoria grabbed the bread with extreme force and devoured the meal as she shoved so much into her mouth that I thought she was going to choke. It reminded me of the village dogs when their master gave them food and they ate it so fast because they didn't want it to be stolen. "Slow down. No one will steal your bread."

Victoria smiled with a huge wad of bread stuck in her mouth while more dangled and crumbs fell to the ground.

"You better go," I said as she finished her last crumb.

Victoria gave me a hug, walked out the door, and hurried across the long walkway and into her room.

Chapter 12

The days passed by in a motionless state of self-deprivation. My body became deprived of my basic needs, and my mind fed constant propaganda about the mission in an attempt to brainwash me into believing in the realities of our goals.

Many nights since being crowned a man and hailed by my peers as a strong and noble warrior, I spent alone in the darkness, weeping under the thin blanket, feeling nothing but an inner child escaping the darkness of the man. I longed for the days spent by the river and wished they could come back to me and allow the youthful behavior to flood and show through the darkened and closing walls. The bland walls, with no color or images that could spur the single spark of a child's imaginations, were all that I saw. The walls depressed me, but there wasn't a single person that could help through the depressed state.

I had yet to leave the compound, but that changed today. The commander informed a few other soldiers that our mission was to go on a three-day trip so that we could get supplies, such as food, beverages, and more recruits.

Waking up early that day, I put on my green shirt, army pants, and boots that the commander presented new soldiers upon graduating from training. The AK-47 propped against the stained wall in the corner of the dark room was grabbed and held to my chest with the barrel pointing toward the casement. This gun was too big, but I had gotten adept at using it. The gun dangled by my side for a few minutes while I scanned the room to see if there were things that I missed.

I felt like a man holding a gun, dressed in military attire, but appearing as an innocent boy ready to step outside into the real world and enter the life of a criminal. My clothes were too big, and my gun was difficult to hold. My face wore the ideals of a child, but I didn't dare think the thoughts as the man inside did not wish to hear the innocent thoughts of a boy.

I stepped outside into the rising sun and walked toward the vehicle that would take us on our journey. There were six of us going with two trucks. The plan was to load one truck with supplies that the movement needed while the other truck carried the soldiers and new recruits back to the compound.

The soldiers and I planned to go to the bush villages because the FRELIMO government had controlled most of the large cities, and it was impossible to overtake the capitals of the provisional districts with six of us. FRELIMO had lost support in the earlier years and only had the labor to control large cities, such as Maputo and Maxixe.

The commander walked over to me. "You bring me back good stuff and don't be afraid to use that gun."

He placed his hands on my cheeks and rubbed them in circles. I looked up at him as a son might look up in appreciation of his father, as there was a strong connection. I tried to resist this notion, but as the memory of my old life faded, and he was the only father figure that I had, I clung onto this idea.

The emotions I felt were torn between the thing I knew was right and the things that I felt I needed or wanted to do. When I held that gun in my hands, masculinity formed, and a boy ready to conquer an adult's world appeared. There was a need that I felt, as I had to leave the compound and experience the action, which was becoming an addiction. I knew it was wrong, but it was what it was.

At the same time, I was scared because of the unknown world that I wanted to vanquish. I sat trembling in the hot sun, with my stomach turning into knots, and the courage inside wanted to cry for the scared boy, but the man didn't let this emotion show in front of the father he wished he had.

The truck was loaded by the soldiers one after another, and soon, we began our journey. Once we left the compound, I realized how far out we were. I saw a large flat land that surrounded the compound, and there was nothing to be seen. There was no home or village or even a farm. The compound was alone, so even if I wanted to escape, there would be nowhere to go, and a slow painful death from the hot sun would be inevitable, walking for miles with no sight of water or shelter. The sights of the parched land, with dead grass and dry heat, brought a real sense of loneliness and abandonment into my mind. There was a glimmer of hope as I noticed off into the distance, hundreds of miles away, a tall mountain with the slightest hints of green lush land. I held on to the notion of that mountain being a better place.

The truck drove for an hour before the first sight of a home. There wasn't even a village with a store or any sight of neighbors. There was a small shack in the middle of nowhere. The shack sat near the road, exposed and vulnerable to passing vehicles. The walls were a brown reed material, and the roof rusted a darker brown, allowing small holes to form. The sun shone on the home, casting a distinct shadow spreading outward, blanketing two young boys playing in a mud puddle created from the night's rain. The children were covered in dark brown dirt, with their feet submerged into the slimy substance; and they were content at playing in silence, unaware of the happenings that surrounded them. The innocent faces of the two children brought a small relief to my hardened exterior.

A woman was hanging clothes on the line to dry. The mother's eyes widened as she saw the vehicle slow. The whites around her iris grew larger as she stopped her daily chores and walked over to her children. Her eyes sagged, and her cheekbones dropped. Small amounts of sweat formed around her forehead as she tightened her body.

The father worked in a small garden. He bent low to the ground. The man was older with a thin figure and back that hunched over and showed a large bump that formed just under his neck. His face wrinkled, and his jaundiced eyes had large bags under them, showing the cynical bitterness of his hard life of work, sweat, and little pay for the fruits of his labor.

The truck stopped to a crawl as we scanned around the house. The men in the back of the truck looked at every possession that the weakened family had. The soldiers looked at the home and noticed that there was nothing around that could be of use. There were a few old pans, half-used sack of rice, and a few plates that were in large blue buckets, waiting to be washed. The garden was not yet producing any food; and the family looked too sick, old, and too tired to be of any use to the movement.

The truck sped up, and we left them be.

We drove for another half an hour before we came to a small village. There were a few stores and maybe twenty to thirty homes that the villagers built around the center of the town. Soon, we stopped the car and disembarked. Children ran away from us, back to their mothers, and the small quaint stores tried to close shop by locking the steel entrance door.

The breeze blew the dirt-covered land around as people sensed the lurking danger and retreated into their homes, only to peek through the dirt-covered glass. Rounded huts made of cow dung and dirt topped with a reed roof, which provided a small shelter.

I glanced over the truck and near the side of the road; a small boy stood behind a makeshift kiosk, where a mom stood, selling cookies and candies for the local children. The kiosk was made of a few sticks, with chicken wire to hold the front in place, and emptied rice sacks on either side to form a small boxed kiosk, with an opened back to enter and exit.

I walked to the mother with my gun now erected toward them. Small packages of cookies sat on a small counter, made of an old rotten piece of wood that provided a small flat surface. I looked through the chicken wire fence that provided protection. The mother grabbed her child by the face and pushed him behind her large body. I reached for a package of cookies and grabbed them. The woman reacted by reaching her hand out, trying to stop me. I glared into her eyes and grabbed my gun tighter, thrusting it toward her. The woman's eyes darted toward me, then lowered, and retreated, allowing me to steal the small treasure.

I walked toward a small shop with a steel door closed and locked from inside the store. Zélio stood near me as we watched a fellow soldier tap the door with his forefinger as if he were trying to send a signal that we wanted to enter. The shop owner had no response. Zélio raised his weapon and aimed toward the hinges screwed tight to the wooden frame. He shot three bullets into the bottom hinge and then three more at the top. He then walked over to the door, with his boot raised, and kicked the door into the shop. Zélio walked in and kicked the door to the side, allowing the echo of it slamming against the concrete floor to linger in the air. The rest of the soldiers followed.

There was enough room for five people in the shop. There was a large counter, and behind the counter were supplies that the village needed to be given by the shop owner as there were no aisles to browse through and take what you wanted. There was a variety of supplies that fed the locals, which negated the need to journey into the larger cities on a daily basis.

"I . . . I don't want any problems," the old, balding, and gaunt man stammered.

The man's hands stretched out toward us in the symbol of retreat. The man's eyes widened and continued to glare at the weapons that were an imposing threat to him and the village. His hands shook, and his face grimaced as he waited for his fate to be cast upon him. The man continued to scowl toward us as he wore vertical lines under his eyes and his forehead lowered.

"Shut up. Give us your food and money," Zélio demanded.

The old man reached for his money but instead grabbed a pistol that he stored just in front of the meager coins that he had collected throughout the day. The sight of this gun caused an immediate reaction. I lifted the AK-47 to my eye and without hesitation let bullets fly toward him, which hit his head and shoulders. The bullets pierced through the body and hit the bags of rice stacked behind him, allowing a steady stream to hit the ground.

He dropped to his knees, and his eyes went blank and stared toward me in a vacant deadly glaze, exposing his whites. Time stood still as the lifeless man posed before me on his knees. A trickle of blood ran down his face, from where the bullet pierced his brain, causing immediate death, and more blood soaked into his shirt and spread out around the bullet hole. As time caught up with the man, he toppled over toward the ground. Blood came out from behind the counter and toward our feet.

"Clean him out," Zélio said toward a few men that now gathered outside the shop. The soldiers began to take bags of rice, flour, and beans. "Nice shot, little man," he said as he grabbed my elbow.

I couldn't stop thinking of what the commander had told me. Don't hesitate with that gun. That is what I did, and I knew that he would be proud of me, or at least now, I hoped that he might.

Bags of food were taken from the store and placed in the second truck. The villagers looked on as they saw their possessions being taken and loaded into a rebel vehicle. I could see the anger fill up in their eyes, but they were powerless, standing with no weapons or hope for a fighting struggle.

I stood by the truck as the last of the bags were thrown into the bed. Zélio and the others then walked over to the local bar. I stood by the truck, but Zélio stopped one of the men and directed him to watch the supplies.

"Aderito, come here."

I walked toward him as he placed his hand around my shoulder. We walked into the bar and sat at the only table in the entire place. Two of the soldiers were forced to stand, but I sat in a plastic chair next to Zélio.

"Give us a bottle of beer," Zélio directed at the young man that stood behind the counter.

The bartender nervously gave each of us a beer and then popped open the bottles and walked away. The bartender wanted to reach for his gun but had heard the shots come from the neighboring store, and he didn't want the same fate, so he left it there and watched the soldiers enjoy their beverage.

The bar was the same size as the previous store but did have a few outdated posters on the wall that each had rips at the bottom. There was a refrigerator that kept the drinks cool, and the table that we sat at was plastic and square. The bar was bleak, with no music, paint, or lively chatter from various patrons.

Zélio raised the bottle in the air and said, "Here is to a successful voyage and to Aderito for his quick thinking and saving my life." They cheered and then in unison took a swig of the beer. This was the first time that I had tasted the substance, and I wanted to spit it out but knew that I couldn't. The first gulp was finished, and I soon took another.

The adults appeared to be enjoying the beer, so I thought that it must be trustworthy, but why it wasn't palatable for me was a mystery. I continued to consume gulp after gulp until I finished. I didn't want to appear weak in front of the men, so I made sure that I was the first to finish.

"Give me another for the road," I shouted to the bartender.

The men cheered at this, and the bartender, twice my age, obliged as if I were king. The rest of the men finished their beers, and then

Zélio directed them to take more for the night. Soldiers took several crates and loaded into the truck.

I jumped into the truck with my beer in hand, and the rest of the men followed. I pulled Zélio over and said, "Are we going to take any of these young kids with us?"

"On the way back. Right now, they will be useless to us and may cause problems."

The engine started, and we drove away from the village, leaving them in the dust that we kicked up behind. At the end of the village, a small child with a fly resting on her lower lip sat, sucking on a small blade of grass. Her belly showed signs of kwashiorkor from the malnourishment of her diet, forcing her stomach to bulge out as if she were a pregnant woman. For a brief second, I sympathized with the young girl as I knew that the food she needed to be healthy was just stolen from the village.

The young girl's eyes filled with sorrow, and her weak body produced a single tear. Her eyes were wide, and her face appeared to have little emotion, but her body expressed a deepened sadness caused by a lifetime of poverty, leading to desperate attempts at survival. I reached into my pocket and found the package of cookies. I flung them toward the girl, who walked two steps forward, grabbed them, and watched as the truck drove off into the distance, over a small hill, and out of sight on our way to the next town.

We had driven for a while before we found a small grouping of imposing trees, which grew in the middle of nowhere. "We'll camp here tonight," Zélio said as he jumped from the front seat of the truck.

The beers were unloaded first. Two men, without being asked, started to prepare a fire while two others started to prepare the food for the evening. The rest started to drink. I found a spot under a tree. My back propped against the massive trunk and a beer in one hand and a crate within arm's reach. I sat, watching the men work, not helping them one bit, as I felt as if I were king resting in front of his men. After the man at the village found his death, people started to respect me as a soldier and not a little boy.

Once finished with one beer, I threw it aside and grabbed another. After each empty bottle was tossed to the ground, my craving for the liquid intensified.

My eyes started to turn around, my head became light, and every time I moved, my body started to spin. I got up from where I was sitting because I had to go the bathroom. I took one step away from the fire and landed right back on the ground, splashing the beer that I held tight in my right hand. My hand was soaked, but I didn't mind as I sat on the ground and could hear faint laughter behind me at the campfire. I began to lick my hand, trying to get every ounce of beer in my mouth. Once finished, I gathered myself again and made one more attempt at heading off into the night's bush to take a piss.

Eventually, I lifted myself to my feet and swayed back and forth. Every step that I made, my body propelled to the right and then left. As I walked further away from the camp, the warmth on my back got colder and colder as my body felt the slight chill of the African night. I reached a place where I couldn't hear laughter from the soldiers and only saw a small flicker of the fire.

I unzipped my jeans and started to relieve myself. As I did, my body swayed back and forth, and my urine zigzagged with the sway of my body. Once finished, I stood there for a few minutes and looked up to the sky. I saw bright stars that lit the ground where I walked. For a strange reason, I had a memory of America. The image was vague, but I remembered looking up at the sky in the middle of the city and seeing no stars, just clouds. I thought how wonderful this was to be able to see the stars. This might have been the first time that I had seen them so visible or at least the first time that I noticed.

An image of my father and mother soon became clear. A small tear formalized as I started to see their image and remember the happier times, which I thought of less and less. Victoria realized this and brought them up often so I didn't lose their memory, but I was. I looked off into the distance, which appeared to be an endless amount of space, with nothing but darkness in front. For a moment, I thought of running. This could be the time when no one noticed until morning. The soldiers were so drunk they had forgotten where I was and relaxed in their drunken mind.

I glanced over my shoulder and saw the soldiers off in the distance. Gazing one more time in the unknown space, I couldn't bring myself to do it. Deep down, I knew that this was my family, and I couldn't change that, so fighting for the cause was what needed to happen. I turned around and staggered back to the camp.

CHAPTER 13

The next morning, I felt the pain of sleeping on the ground, exposed to the mosquitoes and the natural wonders of Mozambique. My head was causing me pain, and the slightest clinging of empty beer bottles being kicked by the rustling of feet near my head caused me to curl in my half-conscious body. My eyelids lifted, and the new source of pain was the beating sun hitting my naked face. I gave a sigh as I lifted my head and noticed everyone was busy packing the truck, unaware that I was sleeping next to the working movement. I rubbed my eyes with my dirty hands and rose to my feet, cracking my bones and exercising my body into a comfortable standing position.

The next town was half an hour away. At least this time, we were traveling on paved roads, where my body could relax from the constant bumping and swerving to avoid the various road obstructions. I sat in the back of the truck, relaxed and content to lower my head and drown my thoughts in the coming day's events. I tried to avoid any loud noises or sudden movements from my head. This, of course, was impossible with the sharp whizzing sound coming from the pounding wind, created by the swift and sharp-moving truck.

We arrived at the small yet more civilized town than the last. The villagers constructed their homes of concrete, and they had a few more shops to occupy the residents. The soldiers stepped out of the truck and started to walk through the street, looking from house to house. Nothing was done for the first twenty minutes, except strike fear into the residents.

Zélio asked that we meet as a group, where he conveyed our mission to steal money, food, and supplies; then go up the road; and return later in the night to take more recruits on our way back to the compound. Once he gave the order, we went from one shop to the next.

I was hungry because we didn't have breakfast, so the first thing I stole was cookies and bread from a local bakery that sold one kind in a dirty glass-covered bin. This didn't bother me as I ate the bread before exiting the shop.

During the entrance into the next shop, I stole rice. The bag was far too heavy for me to carry, so I held the shop owner at gunpoint and forced the middle-aged man to take the rice and place it in the truck. The owner did this without questioning but obeying my commands.

An older man saw that I was a child and tried to stop me. He yelled several times, but I was unaware of his attempt. The old man tried to scold me as if I were his son, but what he didn't know was that my new father praised me for my actions. I allowed the shopkeeper to scurry off, unharmed, as I looked over at the old man, who went to grab a long stick on the side of the road. The stick had several small branches coming off and was as thick as his thumb. I walked over, with my gun resting on my side. He picked the branches off until he had a long straight stick. The man held it tight, forming his weak muscles and bulging out his thick veins. I raised my weapon, hoping that might scare him, but he stood strong, yet looked weak in his aged body.

I approached the man, and when I was a few inches from the stick, I flipped the gun and knocked his hand hard, forcing him to release the cane back to the ground. He rubbed his hand vigorously and looked into my eyes. The man's lower lip shuddered, and his hand shook back and forth.

"Why does an innocent boy look and act so evil?" he said as a single tear rolled from his lower eyelid, shaken by the sight of me. "I look at your face, and I see such sweetness, but there is something about you that shows destruction. Why, my son? What did they do to you?"

"I am not your son, old man," I said, unfazed by the perplexed man who curiously asked questions.

I took the butt and rammed it toward his face, which knocked him to the ground. As he fell, his eyes did not leave my face as he tried to find the child but could only see the bad. He winced in pain as he fell to the ground. His shaking hands covered the beaten stomach, and his lips trembled more as the stricken eyes glared at me, approaching. I gawked at the man as if he were less than human, and I began to kick hard in his rib cage, gaining satisfaction as the man curled and wept in pain.

As I looked at him lying and gasping for air and fearing for his life, I turned him over so that he was looking up at me, dominating above. I lifted my shoe, just above his mouth; and then with my strength, I rammed the heel toward his throat. My lips clenched tight together, and my right hand made a tight fist. Each time he gasped for air, I rammed harder, hearing his front teeth shatter and break free. The man started to spit up blood, which exited his mouth as if it were a fountain running through his face toward the ground where his head rested.

The stick was collected, and I returned to him a second later still lying, spitting up blood but alive for now. I turned him over once more so that his face now rested in the ground. Puddles of blood formed around his face, and his chest rose and fell. The man wept from the pain and pleaded and cried for my mercy, but I had none to offer.

I clenched the stick hard in my right hand, forced the gun to rest on my back, and strapped around my neck. The stick was raised in the air and soon came hard on the man. I stopped and listened to the cries that spread in the air, but no one cared. Repeatedly, I struck his back and buttocks. Over and over, I struck until he cried and wept louder. The man moved back and forth, trying to avoid the bruising crash of the stick.

"Think you are a big man? You are nothing but a little child compared to me," I yelled as each blow with the stick caused a loud scream.

The humiliating words struck fear in the old man, beaten, and succumbed to the fear of a devilish child. The man didn't resist and took the punishment as if he were less of a man and understood the hierarchal power.

I threw the switch to the side and straddled him and then pointed the gun and paused for just a brief second. On the side, a few children stared at the man lying in his own blood, so I pointed the gun toward the kids, who cowered toward safety. I then gave them a wink. I had become what I feared so much: Zélio, the man with the scary face. However, I liked it, because if I didn't, that might mean my death.

The gun went back toward the old man's head as I placed my finger on the trigger and was ready and willing to take another life.

"Aderito, come on, time to go," Zélio said off in the distance as he stood by the car.

I looked over toward him and then back at the man; and then I spit on the back of the head, pointed the gun into the air, and let off three shots. The man cowered and placed his hands on his head but realized that the bullets pierced through the air and not through his head. Leaning over, I said in a whisper yet in a powerful and darkening voice, "We will be back, old man. Next time, you may not be so lucky if you disrespect me again with that stick of yours."

The man cried and said as if a sign of respect and in total submission to the ruler, "Sorry, I am so sorry."

I walked back to the truck, jumped in the back, and then we left.

***

The night came, and I was anxious to head back to the village. I couldn't get the old man out of my head as I knew I should have killed him. I wanted to kill him, and I counted the minutes and waited until Zélio told us to get in the truck.

During the day, we had prepared sticks with fabric wrapped around and doused in gasoline. The soldiers loaded these into the truck and then jumped in ourselves. We were camping three miles outside the village, just far enough that we couldn't be spotted but close enough that we didn't have to travel a far distance. The village appeared to be quiet, except for the bar, which had a few customers.

Two of the soldiers walked into the bar and took several crates of beer. Once they exited, three more men came in with torches. They lit them until there was a ball of fire on the end. The soldiers pointed the guns toward those who were in the bar, shot them without hesitation, and threw the fire toward the liquor that lined the walls and then stepped outside as the building shot up in flames. The rest of the village noticed this, and the chaos pursued.

More flames were thrown at various houses. We tried to throw them on the roofs, which had thick reed material, or on the frames of the windows and doors that were made of wood. People scattered and ran. Gunfire broke out, and the people became target practice as we shot anyone who we wanted.

Two young boys, maybe a year younger than me, appeared on the side of the road. The boys were hugging each other, glancing, scared at the flames that surrounded them. The parents had forgotten them or had been shot. I thought that they might be solid recruits. The boys were my size, and the commander should be pleased to beat these boys into shape.

I walked toward them. Flames of the fire behind cracked toward the sky, lighting up my demeanor as I approached the boys, striding, angry, in their direction. One of them noticed me walking, and they started to move. I ran after them. As we chased around, the smaller of the boys tripped and fell to the ground, scraping his face. The taller boy came back to try to help, but at this point, it was useless as I had now made my catch.

Before the taller boy could look up, the butt of the gun came crashing hard on the back of his head; and now both boys lay on the ground, looking up at me. All they could see was a black figure approaching in the dark. The shape of my body glowed from the fire. I kicked the smaller boy hard in the stomach and then the larger boy, and then I went back and forth between the two until I knew they felt the pain and the discomfort of my boot. I stepped backward and pointed the gun toward their head.

"You are going to be soldiers. Get up," I demanded. "Walk toward the truck and then get in."

The boys did as I demanded. The two walked with a noticeable limp, holding their ribs. The boys approached the truck and jumped into the back. I turned toward one of the soldiers. "Watch these two." He nodded and pointed his gun toward the two boys who now crawled toward the back of the truck bed and propped their bodies in the cab. The boys held each other tight and teetered together.

I walked away from the truck and stopped in my tracks. Men, women, and children became intimidated, as soldiers fired and shot the innocent people in their backs. Every house engulfed in flames. Zélio, off in the distance, had grabbed another child of twelve years old. Zélio pulled him by the shirt, dragged him three hundred feet past me, and threw him into the truck.

I noticed the old, beaten, and bruised man from the morning. I walked toward him as he stood frozen in his tracks, shocked at his village being destroyed. The man noticed me but was too bruised and banged up to run. The old man fell to his knees and wept a few tears as he reached his hands out toward me and clasped them together.

"Sorry, sorry. Please don't harm me."

He cried the words repeatedly as I stopped a few feet in front. The old man sat on his knees, making sure that he was lower than I stood, begging for his life and showing me the respect that I needed and that I deserved from these common folks. I felt as if I were king and he was my servant.

I showed him mercy in the morning, but I knew at that moment that it was a mistake, and he should have been sentenced to his death. Raising my weapon to his head, I held it for a brief second. The man could have grabbed the gun, taken control, and killed me; but he was a beaten man, who was now weaker, and I was the alpha dog.

The man let out one more cry and then pleaded for his life. The old man looked into my dark eyes and noticed the destruction that they had created. The man knew that his pleas were useless as he lowered his head and began to pray. Before he finished, I shot him dead and then watched for a while as the blood soon coated my boot. Deep breaths entered and exited my mouth as I closed my eyes, feeling complete satisfaction that I righted a wrong.

I turned around and noticed that many of the soldiers had started to move back to the truck, so I ran as well toward the first truck. There were five children sitting in the back. I remembered this moment when Victoria and I found ourselves captured. The children shuddered in fear, the same way that I did, but I wanted to assure them that this was the best thing. They would be given beer, heroin or cocaine, and a new family. The children might learn how to be strong and how to be men. Even though they sat scared, wanting to cry, they had found their greatest clan ever.

The truck sped off as we continued to watch the remaining villagers who had gathered in the street as their homes burned from the blazing fire. The fire that emblazed the land shot to the sky and looked wonderful. This looked as if the devil had come from below to capture the village and teach them the best ways. In many respects, we were the devil, spreading fear across the land, and we couldn't be stopped.

For miles, as we drove, I saw the fire shooting high into the sky. We stopped for the night, but we could still see the remaining images of our devilish behavior and demolition, and we couldn't pull our eyes away from the destruction that RENAMO caused that evening.

CHAPTER 14

Rain beat on the rooftop and filled the different holes that formed around the compound. There was little movement among the soldiers. The dreary rain had been pouring for the past few days, with little break. The wind coming from the north twirled the rain around, spraying my face. But the calming sounds of the rain falling from the sky and the subtle thunder from the distant storm calmed my anxious body.

I stood in the small doorframe of the room, with my eyes fixed on a knife twirling in my hand, occasionally penetrating the wooden frame, carving out small notches. I tried to time the thud of the knife with the sounds of thunder, but the natural wonder of the storm was on a different rhythm.

Off in the distance, Victoria had left her dorm and started running toward my room. Victoria bounced and tucked her head into her shoulders in an attempt to stay dry, but the efforts were pointless. A smile formed as she slipped and skidded in the mud, catching her balance but coming close to falling during the attempts. By the time she reached me, water had drenched her body; and mud clung to her bare feet, protected by a thin sandal.

Victoria shook her hair and wiped the water from her face. We stood silent, listening to the rhythmic sounds of the water hitting the tin roof, then rolling to the ground, and the pitter-patter of the water hitting the puddle, which formed next to the entrance. There must have been a reason for the visitation, but I wasn't going to ask because she would tell me when the time was right.

Her eyes looked from left to right and around the room, making sure that no one was around to hear the secret. This led to the aching curiosity, which now gripped my attention before any words were spoken. Once it was evident that no one was around, she said in a soft whisper, trying to ensure her voice didn't echo, "We should escape tomorrow night."

I stopped and looked deep into her eyes, grabbing her arm and holding tight to the point that it started to hurt. Yanking her inside, I slammed the door behind and then looked around the room and glared into her frightened eyes.

"Are you crazy? People will hear. We can't—"

"Yes, we can," she interrupted. "There are fewer guards at night, and we could sneak through the hole in the fence on the far end of the field—"

"And then what? We are miles away from any town. We'll never make it on foot before the morning. There is no money to get transportation, and we don't even know how to get to where we want to go."

"We get the money and then run. We do whatever is needed in order to escape."

"I should beat you for such things . . . better yet, I will tell the commander—"

"Please don't. I was just suggesting." Her pitch rose with panic.

"I won't tell, but you need to stop this nonsense."

"But why?"

"Because our best hope to live, to see adulthood, is to fight for the commander and to make sure that we do everything the commander asks."

"But—"

"No. Now promise me that you won't escape."

"I promise," she said after a long bout of silence.

Victoria was reluctant to say this, but she knew that I was right, and escaping from this place would be suicide. Victoria and I sat on the hard thin bed, contemplating the conversation but scared to go further. I could sense she wanted to continue to prove her point, which she needed for her own sanity. Victoria fidgeted on her seat and many times opened her mouth, ready to say something, but nothing could convince me of the righteousness of risking our lives for the right to freedom.

"Listen, if the time comes and we can do this without being caught, then we will talk," I said, hoping to alleviate the pain of silence.

I said this to plant a small glimmer of hope in the possibility of freedom and to allow her the right to dream. Victoria's happiness meant everything to me, and if she thought for a single second the captivity might be an endless ordeal that could lead to a dreadful existence, then her depression would lead to the end of her life. A chance of an escape meant the hope of a better life, and this hope would lead to a fighter, never willing to give up on a dream.

Victoria smiled at the thought and said, "I just want to go back to my family. It's hard remembering them, and I can't see my mother's image anymore."

Her hands shook as her right hand pressed against her forehead in a veiled attempt to hide her emotions. Victoria's lips pulsated, and tears boiled up in her eyes. Weeping sounds exited her mouth as she must have been thinking of her mother, whom she felt she had lost forever. She grabbed her shirt, wiped the tears away, and then lowered her back on my bed, stripped of the sheets and blotched with stains, which coated the blue-and-white-striped fabric.

"Me too. I try sometimes to remember them, but most of the time, I can't. This is our new family, and if we are to survive, we must accept this."

She nodded in agreement. "Do you ever wonder what our life would have been if we didn't come up from the river?"

"Sometimes, but I have started to agree with our mission and what we are fighting for."

"How can you say this?" She rose from the bed, angry and distraught at my casual tone and obedient words. "The adults have forced you to kill, to be an animal, and you have a soft spot for this."

"When I am out there on the battle front, I am honored to fight for them."

Victoria stepped over to me and slapped me across the face. I grabbed my face hard and turned away. I held back tears, but my emotions turned to anger as I got up, ready to beat her. Raising my hand, I watched her cower to the corner. I couldn't believe that a servant girl had just defied me. This was a punishable act, and I knew that I had killed men much stronger than her for fewer offenses.

My manhood escaped, and I wanted to hit her as the rage boiled inside.

I stopped and looked into her tearful eyes and lowered my hand as I couldn't strike her. I knew that I needed to assert my dominance, but I couldn't. Victoria had meant too much, and the thought of inflicting fear or pain broke my spirits. Other men would have died that night, but my heart was weak for her, and sometimes I understood this and needed it; but today, the thought upset me.

I went back to the bed and took a seat with my head lowered. Victoria got up, placed her hand on my head, and said in my ears, "The adults have made you do terrible things, but somewhere, that sweet boy whom I first met is still here. Please remember him and your parents . . . I know you want to go back to them. Someday you will remember and come with me so we can escape this place."

I longed to cry, but I couldn't in front of Victoria. She released her hand from my head, wiped the tears from her eyes, and rubbed them on my face. "Someday you will remember how to feel, how to cry and understand morals again." She walked out the door and shut it behind her.

I grabbed my face to caress the wet tear of Victoria soaking my cheek. Getting up from my bed, I paced back and forth several times while I clenched my hands together to form strong fists. I moved them around—looking at every wall, wanting to punch—and continued to pace back and forth several more times before finding my back against the far wall, looking at the rain still dripping from the roof. I slid down the wall until I took a seat in the darkest corner of the room and hit my head repeatedly, getting harder and harder.

I began to cry, which turned into a flowing stream of tears. This was the first time I remembered crying. I pictured the men and children whom I learned to beat and kill. I started to get vague images of my family. This place had made me forget so much. When the images of my earlier life did come flooding back, it gave me a false sense of security that they might be looking or praying for me.

"Why . . . why did this happen?" I asked to myself.

As I said this, there were more images of dead bodies surrounding me and pools of blood covering my feet. I looked outside and didn't see an image of rain; instead, there was blood dripping from the rooftops and hitting the puddle. I hit my head even harder—trying to get the bloody images out, trying to flood the brain with positive times—but I couldn't. It was as if my body were tugged by the duality of man. The darkness taking my memories and erasing them with new ones that suited the deeds the devil desired. God tried to fight back, but the negative energy that surrounded me was too strong, and it was taking over my thoughts. I couldn't escape my fate because this might have been a punishment for a past crime or I was one of the chosen ones. In any regard, I felt trapped because I had done something to deserve this. The only thing I thought about was that I needed to keep fighting and to keep strong, and one day, I might see the other side of those walls as a free boy. I am not sure that I should be called a boy again; my childhood had long since passed, and I was a man who killed and, for a strange sick reason, enjoyed the brutality of my actions.

My head hit so hard that it started to bleed, but I continued. I started to cry even harder, so hard that I tried to say something; yet when my mouth opened, sounds of sorrow escaped, and dribbles of spit rolled down my mouth. I couldn't speak, and my vision was starting to get blurry from the tears that couldn't stop.

I breathed hard, trying to control myself, and cried like when you cry because you lose a child or a loved one. In a way, I did lose someone I loved; I lost my soul, and my heart had grown darker.

CHAPTER 15

Victoria and I sat on the high steps leading to the large circular patio. The silence of our words and the complexity of our thoughts were softened by the power of the gale and rain that continued to devour the compound during the last few weeks.

My face lay mesmerized as the rain fell from the roof to land inches in front of my boot. The battering of the flowing water hit the puddle at the foot of the stairs like a subtle beat of the powerful drum. The water splashed, creating a small ripple that spread outward. My vacant mind felt nothing but the soothing sound, which helped the passing days flow by with small yet important form of entertainment.

The tip of my sharp bloodstained knife rested on the concrete step, and the tip of my finger rested on the end of the knife as I moved it back and forth, creating a small cavity, digging deeper into the solid object as I applied more pressure.

The new recruits continued their training. The child soldiers ran, two at a time past, kicking up mud. Those who wore pants found them dragging behind, caking the frayed bottoms. Those who wore shorts turned their dark skin a light brown, and the rest of their bodies drenched in water, with splatters of clay dirt that managed to reach the tops of their heads.

I watched, scanning the long line of fresh recruits as they passed. The end of the line wielded a small child, eight years old, who held a wooden gun above his head. Water dripped from his green hat and exited his chin. The boy shook his head back and forth, trying to rid his eyes of the water that soaked through his hat. The boy's pants were weighted with water and were one size too big for the small gaunt exterior. His right hand left the butt of the gun while his left continued to hoist it above his head. The boy grabbed the waist of his pants and held them, avoiding them falling to his ankles.

The boy who ran in front of us landed his right foot hard on a patch of slick mud. The foot slid forward, causing him to work his way into the splits. He tried to correct his balance with the other foot, but as he lifted his left foot, it caused him to become further unbalanced. He slid forward another few inches before his right foot went into the air, and he found himself on his back, with the back of his head resting in the thick mud.

The training officer came running up behind and straddled the weak boy, glaring toward him, and started yelling, "You can't walk, then fine. Crawl. Crawl, boy."

The boy turned on his stomach, hoisted his pants up, and started to crawl with his face near the mud. The officer followed close behind, yelling for him to crawl faster. His pants kept rolling down his body, forcing him to stop to pull them back up and continue his journey.

As I watched him crawl off around the corner and out of sight, the entire compound stood still and looked off in the distance as we heard several loud gunshots. I stood to my feet and made sure that my gun was at my side and the strap still around my neck.

We didn't know what to do, so we stood ready for anything but hoped that it was nothing. However, the inner voice told me to ready myself for a fight. I pulled my gun forward and checked the ammunition in the magazine. I looked through the barrel of the gun to check my sight; and then I looked off into the distance, from side to side, looking for any abrupt or abnormal movement, smoke, or anything that might indicate the incoming attack.

"Quick. . . FRELIMO has found our base," Zélio came running toward the center of the compound, past the soldiers, and toward the large shed that held the extra guns and ammunition.

The soldiers followed Zélio's lead and raced toward the shed that was located at the back of the building where Victoria slept. The large makeshift building wasn't organized as you might think. Guns stacked on top of each other and ammunition thrown inside in any empty spot. Many lay in their boxes while other bullets strayed from the original packaging, exposed and ready to fire or deteriorate in the changing weather.

Victoria followed.

Many soldiers were passing out guns and ammunition. I grabbed more rounds, placing several in various pockets around my belt and a few more in my jeans. They even gave the new recruits a gun so that they could help fight.

"You," a soldier said, pointing toward Victoria, "take a gun."

He handed a large AK-47 to Victoria with a bayonet attached to the end. I grabbed a bayonet for my gun and then grabbed Victoria by the arm and led her to the side of the building.

"Listen, you point and shoot. Stay close to me, and you will be fine."

Victoria was scared because she had never used a gun before, but now they forced her to be a soldier and learn to fight.

The two of us ran through the thick mud and headed toward where the gunfire sounded. My heart pounded, and my body was aching not because of the sheer exhaustion of a hard day's work but because of the thrill and anxiety of an incoming attack and the unknown number of soldiers that we would soon face.

The soldiers waited only a few minutes before several trucks broke through a large chained fence that led into the compound. Each truck was armed with a dozen men, who were dressed in the same military uniform and carried a gun near their chests. As the trucks approached, Victoria began to tremble. The FRELIMO men opened fire, first from the confines of their truck, hitting no one, but striking fear into our men.

We returned fire, hitting no one. FRELIMO soldiers were still too far away. The trucks stopped, and the men jumped out, including the drivers. They spread out and then moved forward forcefully at our men.

I took a deep breath and then turned to Victoria. We sighed in unison and started to run straight into the action as if we were nefarious psychopaths ready to kill. I fired a direct hit in the forehead of a young man, who fell back with his legs erected in the air before he landed hard on his back, splatting up mud as he slid a few feet to his final resting place. There was no time to celebrate as there must have been over fifty other men that needed to be taken out.

FRELIMO was aggressive. They shot and killed many of the men that ran on either side of me, but I carried on with our mission. My anger raged as my brothers fell to their deaths or lay injured and now grasping their pain and yelling for help. I ran quicker into the battle, shooting at will; many bullets hit men while a few missed. There were so many that I wasn't sure whom I needed to shoot.

I looked around to make sure that Victoria was close by, but she had been lost in the mix. Nothing could be seen through the thick rain and people running in no organized or strategic manner.

I turned and ran in the same direction to where I came. Rain continued to pour on me as I trenched through the thick mud, which spurted onto my clothes. I looked for her, moving my eyes left to right. A FRELIMO soldier had cornered someone, but I couldn't tell who it was because the man was massive with broad shoulders, so whomever he inched closer to with his gun pointed straight out was hidden by the massive exterior.

I ran in the direction of the man, and as I was approaching, he was about to take the shot. A scream was heard that sounded like Victoria. I ran harder, and my strides became longer as I approached him with my bayonet erected forward. His finger was placed on the trigger. Without flinching, I lunged forward and rammed the bayonet through his stomach. I heard her scream once more as the man released the gun. The gun landed in the mud, sinking two inches. He fell to his knees, but he was still alive.

Victoria screamed and panted loudly. Her hands rose toward her head but didn't touch her face. The hands shook back and forth. She couldn't speak as she looked at the man, trembling before her on his knees. Blood came running on both sides of his mouth, and he could say nothing. The blade still lodged straight through him, and blood rushed out of his body and soaked his clothes. I pulled the bayonet out. He looked at the gaping hole in his body and pressed it with his hands. The man's hands became saturated in the dark red substance, and he started to shake.

Victoria continued to let out slow weeps, trying to collect herself, as she slid down the wet wall and sat before him in the thick mud. She curled her body up and couldn't move. Victoria lowered her head, shielded her eyesight from the body with her hands, and rocked back and forth in a ball.

I raised the bayonet over my head. My right hand grasped the gun, just below the bayonet, and my left hand grabbed the butt of the gun. With one continuous motion, my knife came hard onto his neck. The weapon lodged halfway into his neck, cutting flesh and arteries, but coming just short of reaching his bones. The person's body fell flat on the ground and made a splash in the mud puddle that had formed. Blood continued to pour out of his body and then washed away in the hard rain.

I leaped over and grabbed Victoria. She uncurled herself and saw the man resting at her feet. She looked away and stared into my comforting eyes. With water dripping from my face and streaks of blood on my cheek and hands, I said, "Come . . . we can't stay here . . . Grab your gun." I yanked her with extreme force, as I didn't have time to counsel or work through the situation because we had to leave.

I turned and saw RENAMO and FRELIMO soldiers running and killing whomever they could find. Some hid behind the buildings and cars, shielding their bodies from the bullets, while others ran through the mud, showing their bravery and taking their chances to make a quick kill.

It was hard to tell who was who, as they looked the same, as brothers and sisters.

We jogged through the battlefield, looking around us for any FRELIMO men who were within sight. As we walked through the field, I saw off in the corner of my eye a man running toward the two of us. I turned as he approached. He must have been out of bullets as he was content with stabbing me with a large knife that he held in his left hand. I raised my weapon in the air and took fire. I shot three times, yet he continued to run. Every time I shot, it slowed him down, and spurts of blood flew out in various directions. I shot a fourth time as he lunged forward. This shot landed in the neck, killing him in seconds. He dropped his knife and gun, but the momentum of his body flying through the air continued. I couldn't stop him or have enough time to move. His body landed on top of mine, pressing me hard into the ground. He must have weighed two hundred pounds, as I couldn't free myself. The blood from his neck and a cut artery spurted on my face, and I couldn't help but get several large gulps of the warm salty red liquid.

I tried to move his body, but it was useless. I looked around for help and tried to yell for Victoria; but she was frozen, vacantly staring off into the distance, in a deep dead trance, exposing her weakness to the enemy. Looking off into the distance, I saw another FRELIMO soldier racing toward her.

"Victoria, shoot. Shoot your gun," I shouted until she was released from a cold dark spell.

She eyed the man running toward her and then raised her gun in the air and fired without looking into the sight. Everything missed. The man continued in his unfazed pursuit. He waved the knife in the air and yelled, spewing his spit out of his mouth. His eyes lowered, and his face tightened.

"Look through the sight and shoot."

She looked through the sight and eyed the man. She closed her eyes and shot four times; and when she opened, the man fell to his death and slid several feet in the mud, ending up two feet from where she stood.

"Help me get this guy off," I said, wincing in pain from the man who seemed to get heavier.

Victoria rushed toward me and grabbed the man's shoulder and pulled and pulled until he rolled off, freeing my body. I jumped to my feet and found myself caked in blood. The rain, however, started to wash it from my face. Watery blood now ran down my body like a blood-soaked river.

I stood in the rain, looking around, with my chest pumping in and out and water dripping from my lips. Men and young boys ran aimlessly into their death while I stood frozen in time, trying to ponder my next move. I looked around and noticed that FRELIMO soldiers were becoming thin. The movements of those around appeared in slow motion, and the sounds of gunfire were soundless in my echoing ear.

Anger welled inside of me as I found RENAMO men who had fallen to their deaths. Soldiers whom I called brothers now lay lifeless in the mud and rain that washed their wounds. My lips trembled, and my chest became heavy and ached from the inside out. My mouth opened, and water continued to flow over the lips, creating a small trickle of water that appeared to be cascading over like a waterfall.

Victoria hit my elbow hard, forcing my attention toward her. She said something, but my ears muted the sounds, and I couldn't make out her words. Victoria waved her hand hard, pointing toward the open field, and then started to walk as I followed her lead.

The first kill brought the demon into Victoria as the next several were easy. She feared for her life, and the fear forced her to kill or be the one lying in the thick mud, dead. Her hands didn't shake, and she didn't fear the moral or ethical repercussions. She did as every cold, lifeless soldier would do: kill the enemy. They didn't need just cause; all they needed was the command, and their loyalty would dictate their actions. The thought scared me, because she was the one of reason and determination to escape. Was she starting to understand the mission and the ways of being a soldier? Was she going to turn into someone else? Like me!

"Aderito, look." Victoria pointed off in the distance.

The young boy who had brought us entertainment was sitting on the ground, just behind the second cement staircase, farthest from where we stood, leading up to the dining area. The boy curled up, scared and crying in the distance. He hugged an AK-47 close to his chest. The gun erected toward the sky and stood taller than the trembling boy who sat in the mud. A FRELIMO soldier was walking around the patio. He hadn't seen him yet; but in a matter of minutes, the two would come face-to-face, and the young boy had no hope of surviving.

"Hide behind the truck," I demanded of Victoria, pointing at the nearby parked vehicle that half shielded our bodies.

I started to run toward the boy, screaming, trying to get the man's attention. I raised my gun into the air, trying to get a shot, but I was too far away. The man inched closer and closer to the young boy. I ran faster, but it looked as if we were miles apart. The man was a few feet away from the boy. All he had to do was turn the corner, and the two would come face-to-face.

As I ran through the field, bullets whizzed by my head, some landing within inches off my feet. My gun wildly waved from side to side as I held my hands up and ducked my head lower to the ground. I was sacred to be shot and meet my death as my brothers had done, but the adrenaline of my bravery forced my body to move.

The man stopped, and the boy could see his shoes. The man looked around before continuing. As he turned the corner, he saw the boy sitting. The man grabbed him by the shirt and hoisted him to his feet. The boy let go of the gun as he looked into the large man, who did not appear to see a small helpless boy but a small enemy. He held him in the air for several minutes. The boy's pants fell to his ankles, yet the boy didn't notice. He stared at the man's shaveless face, with utter shock and terror filling his body.

The man threw the boy against the wall, cracking his ribs. He clenched in pain and curled his body, knowing that he would die. The man raised the gun, and as if in slow motion, he placed his finger on the trigger and took aim.

I continued to yell, hoping that he might hear, but he didn't. A long streak of lightning struck the land just off in the distance behind the boy, followed by thunder, which sent shivers through the compound. The man paused at the sound but continued his pursuit of the kill.

More lightning struck, and just as the thunder shook the land, I shot a bullet straight through the man's head. He fell to the ground and landed hard on his stomach just off to the side of the boy.

The boy gasped and cried loudly toward no one. He continued this until I came to his rescue. I approached the young boy and lifted him to his feet. I put back on his pants and then held him tight into my arms as I lifted him in the air and placed his face on my shoulder. He cried hard into my body, but I felt no tears on the already-soaked shirt. The small boy covered my exterior, and carrying him was difficult. In the adrenaline of my bravery, I marched on, rushing him around the patio and toward the kitchen where I sat him down and caressed his back until he stopped wheezing and could look me in the eyes.

"Are you okay?" I said in as soft a voice as I knew how.

He said nothing, just nodded at me. I gave him another hug and sat there with him for several minutes. As we sat, the gunfire continued to echo. He covered his ears, not wanting to hear any more, and rocked back and forth, humming a tune of a song that his mother might have sung to him.

Just as quick as the gunfire started, the fire abruptly ended, and the screams of dying men and children stopped. Waiting for several seconds, I got up and ran toward the patio. I peeked over the raised wall and saw many of the RENAMO men coming out from cover, and I couldn't see any FRELIMO men, except a few whom we surrounded. Their guns had dropped, and their arms raised high in the air.

The commander came out of the building where he was hiding and raised his hands, showing the triumph of his soldiers. "Victory!" he shouted to the men, who responded with a loud scream toward the darkened clouds.

The boy got up and headed toward me. I led him out of hiding to join the rest of the men, each covered in blood, mud, and dripping water from their clothes, yet each man was happy. They were happy to be alive and happy to have won.

CHAPTER 16

The rain soon let up, and the rest of the day, we dragged bodies into piles. We made a pile of the RENAMO soldiers, whom we were going to bury at the edge of the property, and the FRELIMO soldiers, whom we would burn, symbolizing a ceremonious victory.

Standing strong in front of the locked door that held the captured FRELIMO soldiers, I knew they were pacing back and forth, waiting for the door to swing open and meet their deaths. They were sweating inside the damp, chilly room; and I felt proud to be given the job to watch them, guard them, and kill them if they tried to escape.

I watched my fellow brothers roam the compound in twos, grabbing dead bodies. They held the FRELIMO bodies as if they were meat, going to be fed to the dogs. They flew them high into the air, on a pile of their dead friends. The soldiers one after the other piled high.

Before the bodies were thrown, the boots ripped off, belts of ammunition taken, and any other clothing items that would prove to be useful torn off the wet bodies. The guns were collected for later use, and a third pile was created for these items.

The slow laborious process came to a halt, and the commander told the troops to gather in the courtyard, in front of the pile of dead soldiers. He then turned to me and gave the command to open the door, which I obliged in a speedy manner.

As I beckoned them to come out and face their punishment, they stood strong, in unity, and defied my order. "I said come out now," I screamed, allowing the shriek to bounce off the walls and stall in the windless air. They still just stood there as if they weren't prepared to take orders from a kid. How dare they? I knew that the dominance that many in the country had seen of me needed to be displayed once more, so my gun was quick to be pointed toward them. I shouted once more, but they cowered toward the back of the room with their hands stretched outward. My patience grew thin at their disobedience, so I shot several rounds, just above their heads. As the smoke exited my gun, they lowered their bodies toward the ground and made their way toward me, with their arms stretched out in the act of obedience. Walking out the door, they stared at the rest of the soldiers, ready to kill them for the murderous rampage on the compound.

"Get on your knees," the commander demanded.

They did as directed and lowered to their knees, looking at the fallen soldiers. The FRELIMO men didn't want to see the pile of bodies, dripping blood, smelling of death, and attracting flies. They found it unbearable to look into the eyes that opened, staring off into the distance.

The soldiers placed their hands on their heads, and the rest of the RENAMO soldiers looked on with their guns pointed in their direction. We wanted to shoot them, but the commander wanted them to suffer, so we held back our urges.

"You came to our property. You have killed our men. Now tell me, do other FRELIMO soldiers know that we are here?" the commander spoke in a firm voice.

The men said nothing. I always wondered why they held back their answers, which led to such suffering. The commander wasted no time. He looked over at Zélio and nodded. The commander stepped back as Zélio stepped forward, saying nothing but approaching the closest man with his eyes lowered toward the back of his head, and then worked his way around until he scowled into the frightened man's face. Zélio punched him hard and watched as he fell to the ground. He grabbed his shirt, lifted him back to his knees, and then punched him harder, knocking him back to the ground once more.

"The commander asked you a question. Do any other FRELIMO soldiers know you are here?"

The man, once again, said nothing. Zélio grabbed a gun from his holster, without blinking placed the gun to his head, and shot the man dead. He fell to the ground. The other men closed their eyes, and their bodies shivered of fear. Zélio grabbed the man to his right by his face and forced his neck in the direction of his fallen comrade. His eyelids closed tight as Zélio placed both his thumbs over his eyes and pressed hard. He continued to do so, ignoring the man's screams until he opened his eyes and looked at the fresh corpse.

"Now we can do this the easy way, which is you tell us what we want to know, or we can torture you and then kill you," he said, holding one man but directing his speech to the others.

The men continued to stand strong in solidarity to the FRELIMO regime who did nothing but give them little food and shelter.

"Fine," Zélio said as he stepped backward. He grabbed the man's hand, held it firm, and grabbed his knife out of the holster with the other hand. The man tried to pull back but wasn't successful. He was, however, able to wiggle around enough to make it difficult for Zélio to make his incision. Zélio looked up at two large men who stood among the crowd and then nodded to them. With no verbal cues, the men stepped forward and held him in place.

Zélio did not ask again but instead sliced off the man's pointer finger around the middle phalangeal joint. The man bit his lip and screamed under his breath. Loud piercing, agonizing screams circled around the sky and shot through the compound. He asked one more time, and he could say nothing through his pain and heavy wheezing. Zélio placed the man's finger in his mouth and proceeded to cut off two more. The man spit out the finger, screamed loud, and cried, begging for it to stop. His screams did not let up as he wiggled for his freedom but held in place by firm hands. Zélio once more placed the fingers back into his mouth, with the bloodied end of the fingers placed inside, allowing blood to trickle down his throat.

Zélio cut off one more finger and placed it in the man's mouth. The FRELIMO soldier bit hard into his own fingers as the torture intensified. He pierced through the skin, and blood was quick to drip from the middle of the dead limp fingers. Zélio paused, waiting for a response other than muted screaming. He continued in this manner, cutting one finger off and then moving to the next until the man had none.

Zélio shook his head and placed the bloodied knife in the holster. He grabbed his gun, pointed it toward his head, and shot him dead. The body jerked backward, went limp, and fell to the ground.

Zélio moved to the next man and stared at him, moving his head from side to side. He held out his hand toward the man as if he were signaling him to speak and end the pain; but he closed his eyes, bit his lip, and said nothing. Zélio took his knife, cut the bottom of his shirt an inch, and then with his bare hands ripped the soiled shirt down the middle, exposing his stomach. He held the knife in his hands. He stepped closer to the man and placed the blade on his stomach. His eyes opened, and his stomach flinched. Zélio pressed the blade harder, just enough for him to feel the pain, but not hard enough to break the skin. He held it for several seconds and stared into his eyes. Their eyes met for a brief moment, and for the first time, they saw darkness in each other. As he stared into his eyes, Zélio moved the knife toward his genitals and stopped just short of slicing through the private parts. The FRELIMO man's eyes curled up. He clenched his teeth and looked toward the heavens. He wanted to let out screams, but he stood strong. Zélio slashed the man once more on the other side, creating a V shape in his stomach, allowing the blood to drain. He paused and whispered into his ear. Once Zélio realized that the answer would be, he shot the stubborn man in the head and moved to the next.

The next man was quick to be shot, and he approached the last man who was still alive.

"You are the last of the soldiers. Will you tell me what I want to know?" Zélio said, getting closer to the man, shouting in his ear.

I could see that Zélio was getting mad at these men for their bravery. He left the man and returned, carrying a long stick that was on the ground just in front of the building that briefly housed them. Zélio removed an assortment of small leaves that branched until he showed a cane. He swung the branch through the air several times, listening to the swooshing sound. Zélio walked over to the man and ripped off his shirt. The buttons flew outward to the ground, as Zélio ripped the shirt from his body, and the man's back exposed to the growing crowd.

Zélio didn't hesitate as he positioned himself behind the man, staring at a smooth hairless back. He paused for a second, trying to scope out the perfect spot. He reached his hand back and with force landed a blow to his back that caused a crackling sound to echo around the spectators. Zélio continued to strike the man one after the other, and each blow became more intense. Every stroke forced the man to scream into the tranquil air.

He fell face down into the mud. Zélio sprawled over the man as if he were a lion looking down on his prey. He continued to strike the back with brute force. The skin soon broke, and streaks of red flesh peeled the skin open. Zélio didn't stop. I thought he was going to beat the man to death.

Zélio wiped the sweat from his brow and looked down at the bloodied man that lay helpless below him. Zélio signaled for two people to come and pick him up to be placed back on his knees. They did so. They held him there for Zélio to look at the man's face. His body was limp; and his head could not hold up on its own because the man had been beaten, tired, and weak to the point that he wished he were dead.

"So can you tell me what I want to know? You do, I will show you mercy. You don't, I will cut every piece of your body up until you die. I will start with the ears, followed by the fingers, then toes, then limbs. And I will finish by cutting your heart out."

Zélio stood there in silence for a few seconds. The man pondered the proposal. Zélio, growing impatient, grabbed his ear and placed the sharp end of his knife on top of it. The man puffed out his chest and let out a deep scream, "No . . . please stop."

Zélio stopped and looked at the man, who wept. "What do you have to tell me?"

"We were driving and saw this place." He took deep breaths, struggling to speak. "No . . . No one knows you are here."

"Good, that is all that I wanted to know."

Zélio held the handgun pressed to his head.

"You said you would show mercy," the man shrieked, with his voice shaking and cracking.

"This is showing mercy," Zélio said as he pressed the trigger and watched the man fall to the ground. Zélio showed no remorse and looked content with the life that he had just taken.

I looked at the man that I once feared, then respected, and now looked at the man who appeared to have no morals or respect for life. I feared him once more.

I never understood why such a simple question with a simple answer should cause such pain. Perhaps the men didn't want to give our soldiers the satisfaction of an answer. On the other hand, they might have wanted to withhold the information to cause our movement and compound to worry about a future attack, or they might have lied.

The bodies were thrown on the pile with the rest of the victims and soon drenched in gasoline and lit on fire. The smell of burning flesh lingered in the air. Black smoke rose to the sky, and I watched as lifeless bodies burned in a cultural ritual to show the victory that we fought to achieve.

Many children carried out the crates of beer and placed them in the middle of where we stood. Each member of our group grabbed a beer, popped it open, and chugged it, as our eyes were content on watching the fire.

Soon, the flames engulfed the victim so that we only saw an occasional limb dangling outside the fire. Several men began to chant and dance around the fire, circling the flames over the triumph of our conquest.

I sat on the far stairs leading to the patio with Victoria. We held hands and watched the men dance in circles. They spun their bodies and moved their hips back and forth in a circular motion. One man kept lifting his knee high in the air and slamming his foot hard on the ground. When his foot hit the ground, his whole body lunged forward.

The young boy noticed that we sat away from the flames. He walked over and sat in the middle of the silence. "What is your name?" I said.

"Calisto."

"Nice to meet you."

I handed the boy my half-finished bottle of beer, and we sat there for several hours as the fire started in a blaze and soon became smaller and smaller until the flames burned out, leaving behind ashes that blew around in the breeze. Once the fire was gone, the sky broke free, the nightly stars filled our view, the bitter cold took over our bodies, and I was finally at peace for the night.

CHAPTER 17

Since the breach of security by the FRELIMO guards, we have been on patrol day and night. The commander told me to keep a close watch around the fence and then to delineate the abnormal happenings. Of course, the job was laborious and up until this point had wielded no results. Every day before breakfast, I strolled by myself, along the far fence of the compound, and did this for hours until another soldier succeeded me from my mundane duty.

This particular day started out proving to be no different. I walked around with my eyes lowered to the ground and my AK-47 dangling by my side. A dirty olive-colored hat that frayed at the brim, long green jeans, and a T-shirt that was a size too small were the only clothes I had to wear.

My body slouched forward, blinded to the surroundings and absorbed in my idle thoughts. My scrawny physique formed goose bumps in the bitter morning hours. The clouds cast over the sun, and the small thrumming of the rain continued to graze my arms and back.

I looked up, scanning the land in front of me, and realized the compound was eerily silent. A slight mist blew over; fog became tenuous as light fought through the clouds over the distant horizon, creating a subtle but distinct pinkish glow. Looking back down to the ground, I began to kick the dead grass with my foot, watching the gentle condensation spread water outward. My mind mesmerized by the simple pleasures of a young boy passing time during a tedious task. The simplicity of my exertion was a semblance to the inner thoughts of toughness that showed through the darkest of moments.

As I scanned the field ahead, I thought a person moved on the hillside and then went still as if a mirage disappeared. At first, I paid no attention to the movement and continued to walk. Thoughts continued to trail back to the hillside, moving as my body became tense, and I gripped the gun harder. It must have been a figment of my imagination, but I didn't want to take any chances. As I continued to walk, my body and eyes positioned toward the hillside, looking intently for any movement. As I approached, I hoped that it was an animal that had leaped and bounced down the slope, out of sight.

I saw something move and then retreat to be hidden once more. It happened fast, but I swore that it was a human head. I started to jog toward a large hole in the chain-linked fence. Peeling back the fence, I ducked underneath and found myself on the outside of the compound. I grabbed my gun and placed the heavy weapon near my eye, ready to shoot whoever the intruder was.

I made my way up the hill. Once at the top, I saw an old 1970s Toyota Corona with various dents, windows pushed out and paint peeling, revealing the metal undercoating. The car sat at the bottom of the hill while two legs stuck out from behind a small tree that stood isolated. I scanned the horizon to make sure no one else was around, and it appeared to be one man. I walked toward the brave man with my gun raised to my eyes and my body crouched, ready to move fast if needed. I walked diligently, moving toward the target, taking my time, trying to be silent. My eyes glared through the sight, and my finger pressed against the trigger, ready for the kill. Once I approached him, I saw that he had a pair of binoculars, but he didn't appear to be military or a foreigner who had lost his way. The man was there for a particular purpose, but it appeared to be a suicide mission.

I walked toward him, amazed that he didn't sense the presence of someone lingering behind until within inches of his motionless exterior; and before he reacted to the forming shadow, I kicked his ribs. The stranger wasn't kicked hard enough to send him curling in pain but enough to send shockwaves through his spine and force him to turn toward me, startled. His eyes widened as he moved away, only to stop a few feet later. The man glared at the barrel of the gun and gasped from the shock and terror of the possibility of meeting my bullets.

I sensed a man with a fearful pusillanimous, who had surrendered at the first sign of a threat. The eyes widened, and the body pounded. His mind raced from one scenario to the next, each one causing more fear to deteriorate into his disposition. The long gangly man who wore spectacles at the end of his nose, with his shirt tucked into his jeans, looking prim and proper, fidgeted with his legs, trying to read my mind and feeling the emanate danger he had encountered.

"Hey . . . what do you want?" I said, trying to show my authority, but I sensed that it sounded weaker than normal.

His hands outstretched toward the gun, nearly touching the barrel as if his hands might stop that bullet from piercing through his soft black skin.

"Wait . . . wait, I am here to help you," he said, lying stretched out on the ground, trying to find the words that might warrant my ear.

"What are you doing here?"

"I work with a local mission, which tries to help soldiers like you, child soldiers, find their families and gain a better education."

"What do you know about my family or where I come from? How do you know I don't like being here? Maybe this is my family."

"Son, I don't think you could like killing people and fight a war that is not your own."

"You don't know that."

I held my gun tight to his face, with my palms sweating and mind confused with the words that he spoke. Confused by this man and his solidarity, I pondered his actions. Was this a joke, or did he have hidden agendas? Was he here to abscond me and take me to a different compound where I could be subjected to brutal beatings and sexual assault? There were far too many questions and too little time to find out the real answers.

"How can you help me?"

"The mission has a home where other former child soldiers live, where we feed them, protect them, and educate them and keep them away from the fighting."

The possibilities of what he said opened opportunities of redemption and save my sinful soul. The image of Victoria entered my thoughts, as an opportunity she longed to receive, and I wanted to offer this for her.

However, I wasn't sure if I wanted to be confined by the adult supervision. I wasn't sure if I wanted to lose power and authority that I had come to love and people learned to respect. Could I leave behind the drugs, alcohol, and killings that I have come to crave as if they were a horrible addiction? The answer wasn't clear, but Victoria wanted this; and even if I decided not to leave, at least she would be safe and free from the violence that had become a part of our life. This was my opportunity! Or hers!

"And you can help me find my family?"

"Yes, we can certainly try."

"I can't leave . . . not without Victoria."

"Who is Victoria? Can you lower the gun?"

I lowered the gun but held my hand tight on the trigger so it could be raised if he went for a gun hidden in his belt, under his shirt, or in his socks.

"How can I trust you?"

"I guess it's a leap of faith. Who is Victoria?"

"Victoria came to the compound with me. I won't leave without her."

"Okay, can you go get her and bring her here without being caught?"

"Yes!"

"Then go get her, and I will wait here."

I walked backward, not able to trust the man enough to lower my guard, and continued in this manner, reviewing the man every slow step toward the fence. I ducked under, continuing to look at him the whole way back to the main compound. The whole trip, I kept thinking about this man and was still unsure if I should tell Victoria and allow him to whisk us away from this place or if I should allow Victoria to go by herself. I even thought of going back and eradicating the man from this earth and then being hailed by the soldiers as a hero.

As I approached Victoria's sleeping quarters, I decided that I should go to the man; and as he said, it was a leap of faith. Taking a deep breath, I opened the door, which creaked and echoed in the room. As I walked into the living quarters, Victoria sat on her bed. She was startled as I grabbed her by the hand. I led her outside and around the building. Victoria followed, but that was because she knew me as a gentle boy, but her face indicated that she was shocked and perplexed about the disturbance that this morning had brought upon her relaxed state of mind, only to be torn into the hectic and complexity of my behavior.

"There is a man on the outside who wants to take us to a safe place . . . away from here."

"Oh my god," Victoria said in a bubbly tone, smiling brightly and jumping from side to side in the air. Victoria's animated gesture and bouncing on her toes put a smile on my face but was going to draw attention to what we were trying to attempt.

"Calm down. This is our one shot."

I could tell that her emotions were getting the best of her, and everyone could read her face and understand that something was happening. This was because few people in the compound laughed or enjoyed the simple life that we led. I pulled her shoulders, covered her mouth, and whispered into her ear, "You must control yourself, or we will be caught." Victoria nodded, signaling that she understood, and I let her go as she calmed herself.

We started to walk away from the building, trying to be calm. The commander saw us walking together, and he shouted out my name from a far distance. I couldn't run or imagine that I didn't hear him, as his voice was low, deep, and authoritative. My heart sank into my stomach as I looked at him. The commander walked over to me and said in a calm voice, "What are you doing?" His eyebrows wrinkled as his eye glared at my exterior, trying to read my expressions. He was suspicious of my behavior as he evaluated each of my signs that radiated from my frame.

I didn't know what to say, and the confused mind had a hard time finding an excuse because I had no excuse for being with Victoria and abandoning my post in the early morning hours as the compound was just rustling awake. I stammered around to find an answer, but nothing came out except for occasional sounds and clearing of my throat. The commander must have sensed that I was nervous and hiding something. As this continued for several seconds, I found that his attitude had changed with the passing time until he was downright annoyed.

"Victoria, go back to your bunk," the commander said, his voice changing, striking fear into me, wondering what he might do.

Victoria turned around and started walking back to her room. She glanced over her shoulder several times before entering the building.

"Now where were you going?"

"Nowhere," I said, hoping that sufficed his curiosity.

"Bullshit," the commander said as he slapped me across the face. The swift hand forced my face to the side. I grabbed it, and tears welled in my eyes. "Now I like you, and you have done impressive things, but I do want the right answer so that we can deal with this. Lying is punishable by death."

The word *death* stuck in my head. If I tell him, he will kill me; but if I lie to him, he will most likely kill me. I lowered my head to find my thoughts. "There is a man out there that was going to take me away from this place." I gulped and then looked up at him with a sad, remorseful face, hoping that he might have sympathy for my mistake.

The commander paced back and forth, biting his lips and hitting his opened palm to his forehead. The commander tried hard to gather his thoughts. I could tell he didn't want to kill me, but he was mad at what I had told him. He stopped pacing and stood in front of me. He shook his head and looked over at two soldiers passing.

"Come here. There is a man hiding on the other side of the fence. Go kill him."

"Was Victoria going with you?"

"Yes, but I had not told her yet. Victoria didn't know where I was taking her," I lied but was convincing because Victoria's life depended on it.

The commander turned around, saw another soldier off in the distance, and signaled for the man to come. He ran to the commander. "Go tie this boy to the tree over there." He pointed at the large tree that stood by itself, just behind my room. The man nodded and took me by the hand.

He led me to the shed where he grabbed a rope and then started walking toward the tree. For the first time, I feared for my life. I was unsure of what he was going to do. Was he going to beat me, kill me, beat me, and then kill me? My stomach churned and my breathing accelerated as images of my fate caused my insides to palpitate and leave my mind blank.

"Hug the tree," the man said.

I did so without hesitating, not trying to run, knowing that I had done something dreadful, and prepared my mind for the punishment that was coming. The man tied one hand hard with the rope and then tied the other hand tight with the other end of the rope, handcuffing me to the tree. He then stood back and watched as I shook and moved my hand, trying to gain comfort from the tight rope burning my naked wrist. I stood for a half an hour. Other soldiers gathered around, and now I stood sheepishly at my predicament.

The commander came back, holding a long stick that he had spent a sizeable time gathering and whittling into a perfect cane.

"This is what will happen to anyone that tried to escape the compound. Everyone here has been chosen to fight in the movement, and if you think you need to escape, then you will be punished. Aderito's life will be spared this once but not before his mistakes are punished."

The commander walked over to where I quivered and pulled out his knife. He grabbed ahold of the lower part of my shirt and slid the knife under, placing the sharp end toward my shirt and the dull end against my skin. The blade pressed onto my lower back made me realize the punishment was imminent, and my body shivered as the fabric cut. He worked the knife up toward my head until the entire shirt tore, exposing my bare skin. He then cut the sleeves and threw the shirt to the ground.

The commander swished the stick in the air several times, testing the ferocity of the implement. As the stick moved through the hushed air, I gulped several times, and my lips and chin quaked. My legs and body tightened, and I was ready to move; but the rope, getting tighter, held me in place. My heart exploded, and I felt a strong need to let out loud-piercing screams toward the crowd who was eager to see the punishment.

"Aderito, you are lucky that I will punish you, a man who cares about you, instead of Zélio, who would just as soon take your head."

Did he care for me? Was this a father-son bond? Could a father whip his son? The word *care* clouded my thoughts. A man who cared for me but beat my backside as if I were an animal couldn't be a father. This made no sense to me, but he was right: it would be better than Zélio beating me until I was dead.

He stepped back and heard the murmurs among the people. A hundred-plus eyes stared at my fresh and clean back, soon to be cut into like meat, cut up as a constant symbol of my sins and punishment. Heavy breaths exited, and I was ready to be punished. I clenched my body tighter and positioned my hands to hold the rope taut.

As I braced for the first blow, a gun echoed through the valley. The savior was dead. I imagined that the soldiers tortured, killed, and left the body for the vultures. My one last hope of survival, Victoria's survival, had gone as quickly as he had arrived; but this might be destined to be my home, with my new father. Confusion continued to cloud my judgment.

The first blow slashed through my skin as the pain was so intense I wanted to scream, but I held my emotions within my perplexed thoughts. The second slash, even harder than the first. A single drop of blood made my back wet and then soaked up by my jeans. It felt like water, but that was impossible. More blood dripped.

The third strike, and this time, I heard the skin tear. I felt the blood drain from my body, and the pain was unbearable. I tried to hold my screams, but the pain was too much. My mouth opened wide, and loud sobs exited. Tears rolled down my cheek; my head flung backward, and I screamed loud into the air. My chest pumped rapidly, and sweat covered my smooth chest while blood continued to saturate my freshly torn back. I moved my head around the tree, where I lowered my eyes and stared at the crowd, amused at my misery. How could brothers be so amused at such a thing? How could a father beat his son the way this man does?

I caught a glimpse of Victoria, who had her arms crossed and leaning back, scowling at the actions, wanting to scream and shout. Victoria wanted to rush in and save me, but she couldn't unless she wanted a place next to me, taking up half of this punishment. I hoped that she stayed because I had lied to protect her, and if the commander found out, I could be the victim of his pistol.

I stared into her eyes. Victoria gave me comfort. I looked toward her as my sister, the one family member whom I loved. Realization hit that a father would not beat his son this way or brothers find amusement in my discomfort. These people were not my family.

The fourth and then fifth blow were less painful as I stared in her eyes and was able to take the slashing of the dense stick, as a man I had now become. Four more struck one after the other, and the cane tore through my skin. Yet the sight of my sister made the pain disappear.

I heard the stick drop to the ground, and loud cheers of the soldiers broke out, which the commander silenced while raising his hands in the air.

"No one will talk to this boy or bring him food for two days."

The commander ushered the crowd away. The thought of hanging there, draining blood, sounded like a cow being hanged by the tree to be eaten later. How might I survive such treatment? The voices soon became faint until I could hear them no more, as I was alone.

CHAPTER 18

I had been hanging by the tree for a day now, but truthfully, I couldn't remember how many hours or days they had tethered me to the tree like the beaten animal I resembled. My body was tired and had given up hope. My eyes drooped and became lazy, and my breathing became heavy. I couldn't feel my body, but the lashes and pain on my back intensified as the day became hotter.

The first day, the rain stopped, and the sun shone through the thin clouds, which hit my back as if it were lava. The pain was too much. I needed water as my body was becoming weaker. My eyes were starting to get faint as I could not sleep in this position. My stomach and chest rubbed up against the tree, causing a deep red rash, which soon broke the skin open.

Ants formed around my feet and climbed up my back. They fed off the flesh and bit my ankles. I could do nothing. The annoyance of the creatures made me furious, yet no one was around to hear my cries. No one dared come close. I screamed at the biting, yet I was alone in my bellowing.

The rain that I dreaded had escaped to a distant land, and I wished it would come and give me something to drink and wash my pain. I prayed to God that he could make it rain. Praying was something I hadn't done since I had been captured. I had thought God had abandoned me, didn't love or care for me anymore. Now I felt a strange wish to talk with my Lord and Savior.

The day's light soon drifted behind the horizon, with the moon shining bright, surrounded by dark clouds. The soothing breeze blew around my back, chilling it, creating light comfort. I prayed harder in my head as I sensed the relief was to come. Looking up at the sky, I watched the clouds move, glowing in the moon's light. A small chill climbed from my feet to my head. A small raindrop fell into the canyon, formed on my back from the flesh opening wide, and trickled through the entire crevice, creating a welcomed relief. God had come back, and I started to pray more.

Rain trickled from the skies, which soon became heavier and heavier as the seconds ticked. It started slow for a while; and then, as if God were weeping at my pain and as if he had opened the skies, the rain started to flow with quick large drops. The rain hit the leaves and then trickled down, providing a small shower. I raised my head to the sky and opened my mouth wide, trying to catch every drop.

As if a miracle happened, the rain hit a leaf toward my opened mouth, and water dripped off toward my stretched tongue. It was a small amount of water, but it was a miraculous relief in a darkened day.

The soothing water hit the gashes on my back, and the blood washed off, which mitigated the pain. The water washed the ants that climbed my leg; the rest retreated into the hole in which they crawled out of, and I was given instant contentment.

Then, as if God had realized that I had enough and did not want to make me sick from the water, he stopped crying. The clouds continued to linger, now covering the bright moon, leaving me to stand in the spooky night.

This renewed my faith, as it gave me hope of survival, and it was a moment that I needed to understand my qualm and confusion. I knew that I didn't belong here, and God had confirmed that with me.

***

The next day passed, and the commander, as promised, came two days later with a bottle of water. As he cut the rope, my legs failed, and I fell to my knees before him. He gave me the water, which I drank fast. The smooth feel of the water rushing down my throat and quenching my thirst gave me an unexpected appreciation for the man. Beaten, torn to shreds, I still kneeled before my demon, as if I had given up my values, and showed undying loyalty to "His Majesty," the king.

"Thanks," I said as I gulped and placed my hands on the ground, trying to gather my thoughts and will myself to stand before him, as the man I once was.

He nodded. "Victoria is in your room. She will take care of you."

I breathed, gathering my strength; erected to my feet; and started to walk toward my room. My feet were starting to gain feeling, but I was weak. I stumbled around, moving from left to right, as numbness and tingling in my weakened body took control. I wasn't able to move my arms above my head without instant pain. Every time I walked one step closer to my room, my back stretched and the skin widened, opening the torn wound.

I reached the front door and entered. The two other soldiers who I now shared a room with saw me and exited. Victoria was sitting on the bed. She had a bowl of water on the floor and medicine that sat next to her.

"Would you like to change your clothes?" She pointed at a new pair folded at the end of the bed.

"Yes."

"Don't put the shirt on because I need to clean your back. Would you like me to leave?"

"No," I said, not even pondering the answer.

Victoria turned her head as I undressed and threw the bloodied wet clothes to the side. It was hard because my hands could barely move. Everything I picked up felt heavy, and it was hard doing meaningless tasks such as grabbing and buttoning my pants. I worked my way through each garment of clothing until my jeans were fastened, and I limped toward Victoria, who still had her head turned and eyes closed.

"I am done."

Victoria got up from the bed to make room for me. I lay with my back exposed. This was the first time that she had seen my back torn and with blood drying to my skin. I did not see her face, but I felt her presence and the shock her face must have displayed.

She got on her knees, dipped the cloth in the cold water, and then squeezed out the excess liquid to make a damp piece of fabric.

She pressed the cloth on my back and then dabbed it across moving in a horizontal fashion covering the wounds. Every time she touched the forming scars, I winced in pain and clenched my teeth, minimizing the desire to scream. She continued this method many times. When she went back to the water to rinse the rag, red blood drained into the basin.

She walked out the door, emptied the water, and came back a few minutes later with clean water from the dirtied tap. Victoria had long strips of cloth, which she dipped in the water, and then laid them flat on my back. She continued to do this until the affected area was covered.

My breathing slowed as I became more comfortable as I trusted her to take care of me. I lay feeling her presence but not being able to see or hear what she was doing. My eyes closed, a warm kiss softened my cheek, and my heartbeat slowed. The two nights of being awake, scared, and exposed had gotten the better of me; and so my body relaxed and went into a deep trance.

Victoria took the medicine and water and exited the room, closing the door behind, leaving me in the dark room to lie until the morning.

PART 4

Four Years Later

CHAPTER 19

Four years have passed since the beating by the tree. I had forgotten how many people I have killed, how many men, women, and children I have beaten to near death and lives ruined. The realities of war had become second nature. I was fifteen years old, and I had done things that most people could never ponder as a possibility toward human integrity.

The commander said that we needed soldiers, so he forced Victoria to fight. Her fragile body made holding the gun awkward and at times less intimidating, but her ferocious face and willingness to let out her anger on the unsuspecting victim overcompensated for her physical presence. I could sense that the anger she unleashed was toward the men who captured her. Although this anger did nothing for the mission, it did keep her alive, and so I said nothing to try to change her behavior.

Victoria and I stood up in the back of the truck. We held on tight to a roll cage that covered the entire bed. The wind blew hard toward our head as the truck went sixty miles per hour through the potholed highway, swerving from side to side, forcing our bodies to sway against the hard-jerking motion of the rough truck that puttered the opened road.

I stood shirtless, exposing the defining marks that once symbolized the embarrassing story of their formation but now wielded the story of my manhood. The once-smooth innocent back was no more, and the child who once sat inside the shell of that innocent boy died by the tree. A cocoon opened with the many slashes and the man created inside, showing to the rest of the world my flawed yet savage story.

The sun beat hard on the truck, warming our bodies, which became dense with the gale blowing hard, swirling around from the fast-forward motion of the beaten truck. There were no clouds today, just a bright blue sky with the bright rays of the sun shining throughout the flat dead land that we traveled.

Five other men sat on the bed of the truck, holding their guns pointed to the sky and their shirts resting next to them. Their heads cowered away from the wind, and many had their eyes closed, avoiding the heat of the day.

Sitting near my feet were six bombs. The bombs had three sticks of dynamite wrapped around each other. Each bomb had fuses, long enough to take several minutes before detonation. The devices weren't laid in the truck with care, and as a result, they moved and rolled with the bumps and swerves of the truck.

We were heading toward a FRELIMO base. We knew that they were heavily armed, and to go into their camp and start shooting might be a suicide mission. Our task was to send a message to the ruling party.

We approached the camp surrounded by a high fence that was made from various metal sheets and chain-linked fences and surrounded by barbed wire circled at the top and bottom. By the looks of the fence, they grabbed whatever material was lying around or stolen, as the fence did not show any uniformity by using the same material.

We lay on the hill three miles away from the camp. I was still shirtless, and the hard dead grass rubbed up against my body, which now sweated from the heat, forcing the grass to cling to me, creating an irresistible itch.

Guards were stationed at the gate and more patrolling inside the compound for any potential danger. Each one had a gun and several knives that attached to their belt. They had the FRELIMO-issued military gear, which included solid-green pants and long-sleeved heavy cotton shirt of the same color. The guards wore a green hard hat that strapped to their chins, protecting them from flying bullets. Even through the professionalism, they showed little regularity in their movement and looked from the outside to be relaxed, more intent on their conversations and less on the potential danger waiting.

"We will wait until the evening, and then we will progress. If we do this now, they may see us and become alert," Zélio stated.

***

As we sat around the truck, the sun began to set. Zélio, who continued to look around the compound in his binoculars, noticed that several officers had gone inside to eat dinner. There were still two officers at the front gate, which most likely never changed; but for the most part, the compound became silent.

The sun soon set behind the horizon, and our visibility became weak. The night sky cast an eerie shadow over the compound as the clouds formed to block the stars, and the zephyr began a small whisper in our ears. Zélio stood up from where he sat and rushed down the short hill to the truck, where the rest of the soldiers stood, conversing.

"Okay, two of us will sneak around that corner of the compound. The mission is to take out the two guards with the knife. Slit their throat. Don't use guns. We don't want to alarm any of the other guards because we are outnumbered."

The two guards in front stood on the other side of a large corner shielded by a large tree. This provided enough coverage that the guards might not notice. The guards positioned themselves far enough from the gate, which could allow them to sneak behind the enemy and slit their throats.

"Once the throats have been slit, we will drive, place the bombs around the fence, and light the fuses, which will take three minutes to detonate. That will give us plenty of time to get away back to our base. You two go and take care of the guards."

The two slender soldiers walked away from the group. They were in their early twenties, and we called them João and Eduardo. The young men were skinny but strong and knew how to use a knife with precision. João and Eduardo were quiet but worked hard and were loyal to the commander.

We watched as they made their way down the hill, far away, from where the guards were standing. The newly formed clouds covered any trace of the moon, so it was pitch black and impossible to see. Once they moved far enough away from the group, it was hard to make them out. All we could see was a faint black silhouette figure moving in the early evening night.

They reached and pressed their bodies against the steel fence and inched their way around until they reached the tree. They waited, sweating through their clothes for several minutes. Once it appeared that both backs turned away from the men, they walked light on their feet and moved toward the kill.

One of the FRELIMO guards turned around and noticed the men sneaking up behind. Before he could alert the other guards or draw his weapon, both men advanced with the knives drawn, reaching toward the throat with his sharpened knife and slitting it wide open in a singular motion. They held the mouths tight, covering any sound that the men attempted to make, as the blood drained out of their bodies. Their hands covered in blood and their emotions rampant with the excitement of a fresh kill soon let the bodies flop to the ground.

Eduardo grabbed his flashlight and turned it on and off several times toward where we stood to signal that the job was complete. We jumped into the truck and worked our way down the hill. The soldiers drove slowly because we didn't want to turn on the lights or rev up the engine. We were on the hill; looking into the compound and turning on the lights would be noticeable and could sound the alarms.

Once we arrived at the front gate, the other men jumped out. Each one of us grabbed a bomb and then ran around the fence on the tips of our toes, trying to make as little noise as possible. We placed the bombs strategically around the fence so that a large section would topple to the ground but not far enough away where we couldn't manage to get back to the safety of our vehicle.

Holding my bomb tight in my arms, I ran around the tree and a few hundred meters more before I found a resting spot near the fence. I placed the bomb against the metal side and reached for a box of matches that were in the front pocket of my jeans. The match was lit on the first try, and I watched for a second as the flame grew longer and wiggled back and forth from the growing wind. The match was lowered to the fuse; and I watched as it caught fire, sparkling and then working its way to the powder of the bomb.

I watched longer than I should have, but once the fear of the blast took control, I jumped to my feet and raced toward the truck. As I approached, the other men soon followed in my chase to jump into the truck before the first bomb detonated.

The last soldier barely had his foot in the truck before we sped off, with each looking at the compound, anticipating the destruction.

We were a few hundred feet away before the first bomb lit up the sky. Heat engulfed my face, and my body went backward as the shockwaves of the blast hit me. Fire and smoke rose to the sky, consuming the emptiness. Soldiers who rested inside rushed out to see the second and followed by the third bomb detonate their land.

The truck got further and further away as each bomb blasted. Each bomb appeared smaller and smaller, and the intense heat became weaker until the last bomb went off, and we could feel nothing and hear only a small rumble from the fierce weapon.

We wanted to see the expressions in their faces and the anger that followed, but no one came to attack. We imagined that the men were running and firing their weapons into the air, making plans for the attack, wondering who or where the men were. They were probably calling us names: cowards, bastards, and little shits. The thought of them confused, scared, and running aimlessly, trying to find answers that were nowhere to be seen made me smile. I sat back into the truck with my back rested on the cab, my arms stretched behind my head and content with the mission's success.

I stayed like this for the next four to five hours until we reached the safety of our compound.

We acted as if we were heroes, without the welcome, as we pulled into the compound and disembarked the vehicle. I stood outside the truck with Victoria by my side. Zélio came from behind the two of us and stood close but said nothing as he looked at Victoria. I was confused at his odd behavior but ignored his presence.

Zélio approached and grabbed Victoria's arm and pulled her near his body. He rammed his lower torso into her. I stepped forward and said, "She is mine. Let her go."

"Shut up, you—I know you don't use this fine girl the way she was meant to be used."

I took one more step forward and grabbed her hand. Zélio pushed me aside. I didn't give up and went again toward them, but this time, I met his large fist that had a solid gold ring, which caused tremendous pain toward my right eye. The large powerful fist forced me to slide on the ground a few feet. I became dazed and couldn't see straight. As my eyesight started to come back, I looked up as Victoria was being dragged by Zélio. She was kicking, screaming, and yelling for me to help. I shook my head, trying to gain my feeling back. I lifted my body to a standing position where I wobbled back and forth, shaking my head and pounding my forehead, until I was able to see, think, and then pursue the two of them.

They entered a room that was vacant and shut the door. I raced to this door and tried to open it but found it to be locked. Pounding on the solid doorframe, I began to beg for it to stop. Victoria's loud screaming enraged me. My nostrils flared, my breathing became heavy and noisy, and my arms and fingers flexed in anger. I pounded harder and tried to kick the door open, but nothing happened.

I walked toward the casement. Zélio had pinned her to the bed. Victoria shook, trying to avoid his kisses. He punched her hard several times in the face. This stunned and calmed her. Zélio kissed her neck hard and then worked his way to her navel.

Victoria stared at the man, helpless to protect her body and weakened by his muscular presence. Her fingers turned into a claw as she clenched the bed hard and vigorously clawed it as her body shook, trembled, and sweated in the hands and arms. Veins bulged out, her neck sprung back, and eyes rolled toward the ceiling.

He took her shirt as she struggled more. He slapped her across the face. Her lips rocked, and a slight puddle of blood formed around her lower lip before she tumbled toward the bed. Nostalgia brought back memories of watching different men rape, beat, and torture Victoria during the early days that we resided in the compound. The same bed and room once housed the horrific memories that I continued to relive.

Zélio ripped the shirt in two, exposing her newly formed breasts. Her head still turned, and her eyes released water that mixed with the blood that continued to drip from her mouth. Her breathing intensified, and I could hear the small whimper from the room.

He worked his way to the pants where he unbuckled them and slid them to her ankles. Victoria looked withdrawn and ready to take what he gave. She was tired and had given up the fight. He lowered her underwear, and now she lay exposed. I pounded on the window. Zélio gave no response, but Victoria looked over to me. As she had done for me during my beating, I did for her as Zélio had sex.

Victoria screamed as he moved it faster and faster. I continued to pound the glass, pleading for him to stop. He didn't. I pounded the window until it broke in several pieces, leaving sharp edges reaching from the casement frame. I reached my hand through, trying to find the lock that held her captive, but I couldn't find anything. My arm rubbed hard against the glass, grinding my flesh and piercing it through the jagged glass, releasing a solid fast-moving stream of blood that dripped on the inside wall. I let a single tear fall on my cheek as I saw him release his penis. He looked at Victoria, who lay, avoiding eye contact with the man who raped her. Zélio turned around and exited the room.

He looked over at me and stared into my eyes, which were full of rage.

"She was mine."

"Tough. You didn't use her like a man. Consider that a lesson. That is how you use your bitches."

He walked away, and I entered the room. Victoria lay with her legs spread, weak and tired from the experience. The flesh of her vagina tore, releasing a small amount of blood as wet as the river we once enjoyed. I walked toward her, trying to comfort her, but I couldn't—not yet—so I stepped back. I didn't know what to say. How was I to comfort a girl who had been beaten and raped again? I stood there for a while, watching her chest rise and fall to the beat of her deep breaths. Sweat beaded on her face. She didn't dare look at me but felt my presence. I could see that she was embarrassed and ashamed. This was not her fault. She wasn't being punished; she was a victim. I wanted to tell her this. I was desperate to find the words, but nothing I thought of sounded right, so I stood in the dark room, silent.

Confused at the sight, I stepped forward, grabbed her panties, slid them back over her body, and did the same with her pants. I tried to cover up her embarrassment and give her back her dignity. I grabbed the torn shirt, covered up her breasts, and sat beside her on the bed. The best thing I could do was comfort her, hug her, and show her that it was okay and that I didn't lose respect for her.

I placed her head on my lap and caressed her back and forth. I wiped away the sweat and then rubbed her back. She turned to her side, placed her hands under her head, and snuggled up onto my lap. I continued to comfort her but continued to do it in complete silence.

CHAPTER 20

Victoria leaned against the dirty wall of my bedroom. Her eyes painted with a dark ring around the bottom due to her inability to sleep the last few nights. She had a pained gaze, staring off into the unknown distance. She rested one hand near her mouth where she bit her fingernails out of nervous habit.

Her stomach bulged out as she was now eight and a half months pregnant. She caressed her belly with the other hand, which showed under the tight-fitting shirt, touching the powerful kick of the child that lay peacefully in the womb. The last few days, she paced, contemplating the actions and the events that led to the untimely pregnancy. She worried about every kick and pain to her stomach and walked into the room to witness her crying, worried over the birth and caring for the baby for the rest of her life.

I sat on a plastic chair that had the back broken in two, making it near impossible to lean, so I leaned forward, staring at the floor. I bit my lower lip and pinched my forehead with my fingers. Heaviness was in my body, and my chest felt tight every time I thought about the new baby who would enter this world.

Confliction with my duties toward the baby consumed most of my day. I wanted to help, for Victoria, but the baby was not mine; and therefore, I was uncertain of the time and commitment that I could spend on raising a child. The last few days, I couldn't make eye contact with Victoria or find words to comfort her. There was a need to verbalize the internal conflict and seek the pros and cons of the situation, but I was alone, and there was no one to understand my needs. Confusion, frustration, and anxiety consumed the last few days. I couldn't sleep or ponder the correct outcome.

"What will I do when the baby is born?" she said in a soft-spoken voice, pinching her upper nostril with her thumb and forefinger.

"I don't know. Maybe they won't have you fight anymore."

"That may be wishful thinking."

Zélio, since learning that she was pregnant, never came to her. He didn't look at her and made it abundantly clear that he wouldn't help raise the child. The absent father responded as if he didn't make any mistake and was in denial of his responsibilities toward his baby. When he passed the various walkways in the compound, his eyes lowered and stared at his hands. When confronted, he was quick to make excuses and turned to denial, refusing to respond further, which led to his backing off, walking away, and not returning for several more days. Eventually, I stopped and left him to ponder his mistakes and look into his own inner morals.

We were both children and were going to have a hard time raising a baby. Victoria and I looked toward the future at the possible damage that we could inflict on the baby and our own dim chances of survival. There was a constant rumble in my stomach at the thought of bringing an innocent child into my own demonic presence in the cruel and unsavory world. I hoped and prayed to God that it might work out but knew deep down that the baby would grow in an unstable environment and witness atrocities that could become a normal way of life. What life was this for a child?

The baby was due in a few weeks. We asked Wanga, a woman who lives in the compound and who has given birth before, to help with the delivery. She agreed, and now we just waited for it to happen.

I could tell that Victoria worried herself because the last few weeks she was asking one question after another with no answer.

Wanga was a patient woman who came to the compound a few short years ago in search of food, shelter, and protection. Wanga was one of the few women the men shared and passed around among each other. She often confided in Victoria that she thought she carried HIV/AIDS, but going to the hospital terrified her. Finding out such a thing meant that she might be treated like an outcast and forced to fight the disease on her own, most likely starving and then rotting in the deep African bush for the vultures to take her flesh.

The thought made her queasy, and so she kept quiet and continued to sleep with any man who requested the service, passing the disease from one person to the next.

Wanga always wore a covered scarf around her head to cover up the balding and burning that she experienced as a young child from gasoline being poured and lit on fire by her alcoholic father who found pleasure in the discipline of the household. The scars on her head formed deep sadness and cynical behavior that have led to deeper depressions, which she healed through constant isolation. She always wore a long-sleeved shirt and long pants to cover more scars that were caused from the burning and knives that cut the flesh from a rough and traumatic childhood that she rarely talked about but allowed the deep pain to fester. This pain boiled over, and a dark, cruel woman showed and became violent toward those who punished and degraded a broken and sometimes-mad woman.

Yet through the pain and depression, she spoke to those she trusted. Victoria was one such person. They saw the trauma that each other had experienced and understood a deeper connection and understanding of the needs and desires. As she was being accompanied by Victoria, smiles and laughter broke out, allowing the good to overpower the evil that lurked deep within, finding ways to peek its ugliness. This lasted a short while before the sullen and bleak woman overpowered the duality of her emotions and went once more to enter her demon-filled life, trapped between the hell she lived and her existence on the planet.

The few weeks leading up to the expected due date was hard. It was hard for my mind to stay focused and even harder for Victoria. I tried to keep her on the bed and rest, but her nervous energy drove her to her feet, trying to do work and keep busy. Her stomach had grown several inches, and the baby now was getting restless and ready to come out.

***

A few weeks later, we were sitting on the bed. I didn't want to leave her the last few weeks in case she needed something or the delivery was starting. A checklist kept forming in my mind of everything that I needed to do while Victoria went into labor. It was only a few things, but I didn't want to make any mistakes, so I festered upon my duties.

As we sat, the bed became wet. Water poured out and soaked her pants. She looked around, confused. I noticed nothing at first until I glanced at her, looking around at the water that extended outward and dripped to the floor.

"The baby is coming?" I said in a tight voice as I got up from the bed and paced back and forth, watching as the checklist escaped my mind, and I couldn't recall the first thing that I should do.

She panted in and out. Her stomach rose and fell to the same rhythm. She clenched her teeth tight together and screamed under her breath, not allowing an exit for her painful cries. Victoria grabbed the dirty sheets and pulled them tight, pushing hard, hoping that the child would exit, but nothing came.

I rushed out the door in the hot summer day and through the long road where Wanga was standing, talking to a few other girls. I grabbed her hand, pulled her toward me, and then ran back down the road, holding her hand as I explained what was happening. When she realized the situation, she started running faster.

We entered the lit room, with one bulb flickering over the head where I left Victoria. She managed to take off her pants and underwear, exposing her wet vagina. She continued to breathe and screamed at every contraction. Beads of sweat lay still on her forehead. She grabbed her knees and pushed hard, but the child was not ready to come.

Wanga dropped to her knees. I went to Victoria and dropped to my knees at her side, grabbing a towel on the floor and wiping her forehead clean. I grabbed her hand and kneeled on the ground, wiping more sweat from her head. Sweat drenched her clothes and softened her hair. Her mouth opened wide, and loud booming screams exited.

She pushed hard and gripped my hand. It felt as if she were trying to break me as she squeezed harder with every push and contraction. My face winced in pain, and my body tightened as I tried to resist the bone-crushing trauma. She got tired, let go, and rested, panting stiffly.

Victoria pushed repeatedly, but the baby didn't pop out. She lay for hours before the contractions became closer and closer, and her cervix was dilated. After hours of screaming and pushing, she was growing tired and was praying the baby would come soon.

"I think we are ready. Push hard," Wanga stated as she reached closer to grab and pull the baby.

Victoria let out a loud scream. She opened her mouth and continued to push hard. Her feet were resting on the lower part of the bed. She pushed hard on the steal bed frame, but nothing came out. She pushed again and still nothing.

"Give me one more push," Wanga said.

She did so. This time, the tip of the head appeared. She gave another push, and soon, the shoulders appeared. She continued this until the shoulders and soon the entire little body fell into the arms of Wanga. The baby began to cry, releasing the excess fluids. Wanga handed the wet traumatized baby to Victoria. The baby's head covered in bloody fluids. His eyes closed and hands clenched tight, moving back and forth. Victoria covered in sweat, panting hard from the tiring experience. Yet she laughed when she grabbed the sweet, innocent baby and held him tight to her chest. The baby felt the warmth of her mother, and Victoria felt the beat of the baby's heart pounding. The baby who lay connected and warm settled in a deep sleep, resting just above his mom's breasts.

I rubbed the head of the naked baby, new to the world and without the comforts of a blanket to keep him warm, just the warm hug and embrace from the new mother, who laughed and smiled wide at her creation.

Wanga left the room, without saying a word but satisfied with the result. I looked in astonishment at the gift of life. The baby was born into the struggle, fighting, and poverty that defined us as people. Yet today, the struggles outside and the killing that surrounded us were second to views of the baby sleeping peacefully in his mother's arms. Today was a blessed day, and we knew it. The baby was created from a dreadful scene of rape and violence and may have been born and lived in the womb of the guns sounding and bombs flying. This baby may have lived through so much and may live through what we have become to know as a living hell, but today was just right in so many ways.

CHAPTER 21

A week had passed since the baby was born. Victoria, for the most part, stayed inside, breast-feeding the child and bonding with her new baby, shielding him from the cruel outside world. She named the baby after me, Aderito Jr., which was an honor; and I took deep pride in the baby, whom I had not helped create but had a desire and obligation to help raise to be strong.

She took her first steps outside and shared the world with God's creation. I stood beside her as people looked yet didn't receive her with a warm welcome that she envisioned.

The commander walked over to the two of us and said with neither showing remorse nor looking at the baby that lay in a deep sleep, "Tomorrow, you two will go to a town. Your task is to take more recruits for the fight. There may be FRELIMO soldiers there, but you and the others should be able to take them."

The commander walked away a few feet before I drew his attention back to Victoria. "What about the baby? What will Victoria do with the baby?"

"Tie the baby to the back and go out and fight," he said in a penetrating voice as if the thought of a baby soldier did not bother him.

"But—"

"Are you going to defy my order or question my command?" the commander said, stepping toward me.

Victoria placed her hand on my arm and shook her head, signaling for me to stop.

"No, sir," I stated, stepping back, signaling my retreat.

The commander left.

"I guess I'll have to fight . . . I will be fine."

The idea annoyed me but not more than Victoria's willingness to grab a gun, soon after birth, and strap a week-old baby, dragging the naive child into the battle. How could she say this with little anger or emotion in her tone or body language? I walked away frustrated—stomping my feet, kicking dirt as if I were a child on a tantrum—and back inside my room to gather my thoughts.

***

The morning came far too quick. Victoria had the baby tied to her front with a *capulana*. The baby's whole body wrapped tight from head to toe and lay asleep, gripping the mother's breast. She sat in the truck, rubbing and gazing at the baby, attempting to shield him from the wind the truck created as it whizzed through the bumpy dirt road.

Her eyes did not leave the sleeping child who was unaware of the events that were to come. Her gaping eyes suggested an intense fear and disbelief. The mother's need to protect the child overwhelmed her as she contemplated the actions needed to fight in a battle yet the nurturing and love needed to comfort the offspring. It was clear through the vacant expression that the choices that were presented to her wielded anger and anxiety.

I feared for both of them. Deep sadness and anger filled my small-pebbled heart. The anger burst and pained me, but the helplessness consumed my thoughts. My dryless eyes wanted to cry and release my pain, but the cold body that cocooned my warmth was in a state of emotionless behavior that could not break free to feel the pain of a normal child. I sat and contemplated Victoria and the child but could execute nothing else.

We soon arrived at the small city, as Victoria exited the truck. She grabbed the Ak-47, which she had left behind as she shielded the child with both hands upon the abrupt exit.

"Listen, I will stay right behind you. I will try to shield the baby."

"Okay."

A fabric that Mozambican women wear and use for multiple purposes.

Victoria leaned the gun against the truck; positioned the baby on her back; ensured that the capulana tied tight, protecting Aderito

Jr.; and then grabbed her gun once again and walked away from the safety of the parked vehicle.

We walked around with our guns drawn, watching people cower into the security of the shops. There were no FRELIMO men or women in sight, but as we turned around the corner of the main street, we saw a truck coming toward us. Perched on the top of the truck was a FRELIMO soldier, holding tight to a tripod machine gun attached to the hood of the vehicle. The driver skidded to a stop as he saw us. Behind the first truck were two others, full of men. There were a dozen men in each truck. I counted around thirty-six to our eight and one baby.

My heart started to pound, as I was scared for Victoria and the child. We ducked behind the crumbled building one more time as the man behind the machine gun started to let rounds fly toward the general direction where we hid. The bullets ripped through the buildings, crumbling more cement and bricks around our feet, and the baby started to cry. The sounds of the bullets flying in our general direction, one after another, sounded like loud thunder from the sky. The baby's shrieks grew louder; and soon, everything around me became mute except for the pounding cry of the innocent child, wanting desperately to be protected.

I took two deep breaths, reached into a pocket in the belt around my waist, pulled out a hand grenade, and then pulled the pin. I looked around the corner and threw a grenade toward the truck. It bounced several times and rolled a few feet under the front end of the truck until it rested before the loud blast crumbled a crater into the paved road. The truck went vertical into the air and toppled over performing a 180-degree flip, landing on top of the machine gun operator and trapping the driver in the car.

The men on the ground didn't appear to be fazed by the explosion, and they continued on foot toward the RENAMO men hiding behind the building. Several FRELIMO men took cover behind the exploded car and started to fire their guns, hoping for a reaction from our men. We stood for several minutes, chests puffed out, and waited for Zélio to give orders.

Bullets continued to ricochet off the building several inches away from my head. I held my gun tight to my chest and rested my head against the brick wall, praying in my mind for the courage to protect those I loved.

"Cover me while I try to go across the roadway to hide behind that building. Then we attack them on both sides," Zélio yelled the words, but the ringing in my ear softened the command.

We nodded, and Zélio and Eduardo ran across the road, bullets coming within inches of the brave men. I turned the corner, exposing just one shoulder and the gun, and fired the weapon. I held on the trigger, trying to force the soldiers to retreat and at a minimum force the attention toward my gun and not on Zélio and Eduardo. Out of bullets, I wasn't able to hit anyone, so I retreated behind the building to reload and watched Zélio reach the other side.

A few more RENAMO soldiers on our side stepped forward and continued to fire at the FRELIMO men. A few more opposition soldiers fell to their deaths, but there were too many who were still alive. Victoria took her turn and stepped forward, firing her gun, with the sounds of a baby crying in her ear. She wanted to comfort her child but knew that meant the death of them both. The preoccupied mind missed as the bullets pierced through the tarred road just in front of the hiding men.

"Come." I grabbed her hand.

We left the men there, still fighting. I grabbed the butt of the gun and smashed it through the glass door of the corner store. I ducked through the broken glass and led Victoria into the building. There was a large window on the side street where the FRELIMO soldiers covered behind cars. I smashed it and ducked behind the small section of the wall that stretched from the base of the glass to the floor. I popped my head over and fired several rounds, managing to hit a soldier in the head, and then went back to hiding. Victoria did the same thing but missed in her attempts.

We hid behind the wall as we heard gunfire in multiple directions. I popped my head back over, just exposing my eyes, and looked over to Zélio who was standing, firing on the enemy. Gunfire and smoke came from that direction, and then Eduardo fell to the ground from a bullet to the back of his head. A FRELIMO soldier progressed forward from behind Zélio. I thought about yelling or maybe grabbing my gun to shoot him dead, but instead, I watched as the man inched closer.

Zélio turned and tried to take aim, but before he could get his weapon ready to fire, there were two quick shots. The force of the bullets going through his chest propelled him backward. He fell into the streets, exposed to the rest of the FRELIMO forces. Zélio lay with his arms outstretched, waiting for someone to rescue him, but no one came. He cried and pleaded as he stared at the many guns firing at his men. His eyes grew desperate and darted back and forth, and for the first time, the man who showed no fear appeared to be weak and not ready to die. Zélio reached his hands forward and attempted an escape but weakened by the bullets and the loss of blood that streamed behind him.

The man who had shot him took aim and shot him once more, this time landing the bullet in the back of his head, leaving him lifeless, in the unceremonious pool of blood, exposed to the vultures that would soon take his carcass.

I ducked behind the wall and panted, holding my gun tight to my chest with the barrel sticking above the aperture.

Outside, in front of where I sat, were four other men trying to return fire on where Zélio was shot. They fought valiantly, but more FRELIMO men appeared and returned fire. One after the other, my brothers fell to their deaths until Victoria and I were the only ones left.

"We need to go—now," I said in a desperate and weak voice.

The FRELIMO men were closing in around us. There was a second door at the far end of the shop. We ran toward the glass door. Victoria turned the baby so that it was now resting near her chest. I shot the glass, which splattered around our frantic bodies, and broke through the door, landing back in the streets. I looked to the right and saw the FRELIMO soldiers walking toward us. We started to run, which caught their attention, and they started to fire. Every bullet missed us by a narrow margin. Many hit the ground just at our feet, and others shattered glass, forcing our heads to take cover from the small glass that broke around our feet. I grabbed Victoria's hand and pulled her along the stretch of dirt road. The FRELIMO soldiers chased after us on foot while several more went back to get the remaining trucks, left around the corner.

We reached the truck, which I jumped inside and relieved to see that the keys were still in the vehicle. I started the car, glanced up, and saw them getting closer on foot. I put the car in gear, flipped a quick U-turn in the middle of a deserted road, and started to head out of town. I saw the men chasing the car on foot and felt relieved that we made it.

In the rearview mirror, many trucks came from behind; and the men on foot jumped in the trucks, which sped off toward our vehicle. I pressed on the pedal but barely saw over the steering wheel, and as a result, the car swerved from left to right.

The other vehicles caught us as I tried to go faster, but it was useless. Bullets started to whizz toward the car and broke the back window. We ducked at the sounds of the breaking glass. Victoria placed the baby on the ground of the vehicle and grabbed the gun. Shielding herself from the bullets by the seat, she propped herself on her knees and returned fire, out the shattered window. She killed two people, who flew off the truck, while another bullet hit the front, forcing the vehicle behind to swerve. The driver of that truck turned the wheel sharp to the left but turned it too fast, and the car rolled several times. Clanging and crashing of metal on the deserted road sent relief as one vehicle crashed, and the men who occupied it went flying and crushing the driver until the car rested on its top.

The truck right behind swerved to miss the crushed vehicle and pulled closer. A few men who remained held their guns straight and tried to point and aim, but the subtle bumps on the road made it difficult. I turned the steering wheel sharp toward the vehicle and rammed them hard into the side and saw sparks spread out from the metal rubbing against metal. I rammed them a second time, and the car swerved, knocking the passengers out of the side.

I continued to ram the vehicle to my side, trying to get the driver to flip, while Victoria tried to shoot the tires of the third car, which still trailed.

Up ahead, I saw a bridge. I remembered crossing the bridge. There was a small river and a twenty-foot drop. I rammed the car harder and continued to do so, trying to push the vehicle off the road and over the edge. The bridge was a hundred yards away. I needed the vehicle to topple over the bridge just at the beginning where there was an opening. I was winning the battle. The bridge was closer. I took a deep breath as the two cars rubbed against each other and revved the engines. The bridge approached, and the FRELIMO vehicle rammed into the side. The force of the impact killed the driver and turned the car in 180 degrees. The back end of the car slid down the embankment into the river, forcing the women and children, washing clothes, to flee for their safety.

I took a deep breath as the car passed the bridge but remembered one more truck still trailed. Victoria continued to shoot at the vehicle, but there was too much movement. Victoria loaded the gun with the last rounds of ammunition that we had. She took fire again, but the truck inched closer and closer.

Victoria had three bullets left, and she took aim and fired. They landed in the tire, forcing the driver to swerve sharp from the instant result of blowing a tire. He tried to correct the wheel but started to head toward the tree. He tried to correct once more, but it was too late. The truck hit the massive tree trunk, and the blow of the impact forced the truck to smoke. The driver exited the vehicle and fled to the safety of the open plains.

I continued to drive straight for ten miles.

Victoria picked up the baby and rocked him back and forth. She talked and sang a few songs. The baby stopped crying and fell asleep.

I slowed the vehicle and pulled over to the side of the road.

"Now what? Where do we go from here?"

"I don't know. Where is the base?" Victoria said, continuing to rock the baby.

"Somewhere over there. I think if we continue straight, this road ends, and then we turn right and follow that road until we reach the base."

"I think it is best if we go there. We need to regroup."

"You know, we can escape."

"Yes and how far will we make it without food, gas, and shelter? And we don't know where to go."

"Maybe it would be best to have a plan before we go and make fools of ourselves."

I started the car back up and headed through the bumpy dirt road toward the paved road and straight to our camp.

CHAPTER 22

I was lying on my bed when Victoria came barging in and straight to where I lay. She looked around to make sure that we were alone, which we were. The baby tied to her back, and Victoria distraught as her eyes lowered and roamed around the room and her hands fidgeted and palms sweated. Victoria rubbed her hands on her jeans and clasped them together. She paced back and forth, biting her fingernails and rubbing her ratty hair out of her eyes.

Victoria paced in the darker corners, hiding her face. Her breathing became heavy, and I saw small tears exit from her eyes and land on her face.

"What's the matter?" I said as I got up from the bed as she took a seat, with her hair dangling in front.

"We need to get out of here," she said, brushing her hair aside and wiping the sweat away that started to form. She gazed over at me, and I saw a dark black ring around her bulged right eye.

I sat down and leaned forward, placed my hand on her left shoulder, and sympathetically stated, "What happened?"

She panted and looked around the room. I could tell that it was hard for her to get out the words that she needed. "I was raped again. They threw my baby aside." She began to weep and cry into her hands. "They raped me in front of my baby," she said with her mouth opened wide as the words screeched out, echoing through the small room.

The sounds of the words were deep and hurting to her. Her chin shook, and her head and neck lowered, shrinking into her shoulders, which moved, as she couldn't stop crying. She gripped her shirt tight and tugged it, trying to rip the tattered rags out of a fit of rage.

"Hey, be strong. Be strong." I sat closer to her and gave her a side hug. I started to caress her back and lean forward to show her that I cared and to try to get her to stop crying. The veiled attempt weakened by the loud and constant whimper.

After a few minutes, she was able to gather herself. She took several deep breaths and looked into my eyes. "We should have left when we had the chance."

"It wasn't smart. We had no money, we had no idea where we needed to go, and we needed to recoup. It was the smart thing to do."

"What about now? Is it the smart thing to stay?"

"No."

"Then we need to go."

"Okay . . . I think I can get some money from the safe. I can also get some guns and ammunition."

"Okay . . . when will we do this?"

"Tonight, when everyone goes to bed, come get me from here. Make an owl sound from the outside. I will come, and we will go."

"We will need to get past the guards."

"No, the guards won't patrol the far end of the fence where there is a hole. We can escape through there, head down to the road, and go from there."

"Okay . . ."

"We now have a lot of work to do. We tell no one, and we don't act any different," I said, ending the conversation by getting up from the bed and opening my door, signaling for her to leave.

I waited several minutes until she left; and then I casually walked out of the door, up the stairs to the deck where we ate our meals, and straight across into the main living quarters. There was a refrigerator on the far side, surrounded by a counter that had plastic laminate peeling off, exposing the rotten wood that lay beneath the thin layer. I grabbed a beer and opened the bottle with the opener that was sitting on the counter. I left the communal room and turned around the corner where there was a long corridor. At the end of the corridor was the commander's office. There was a safe in the office, and I knew that in one of the drawers of his desk was a key that manually bypassed the combination.

I glanced down the long dark corridor but couldn't see or hear anyone coming from the office, so I started to walk lightly on my toes. As I approached closer to the eventual crime scene, I stopped as I heard a voice come from his office. I crouched lower and started to back up when his tall frame came into sight, showing only his back as he conversed on the landline phone.

Turning around, I went back to the living room and sat on the couch, continuing to drink my beer. I knew that once he left his office, he would be forced to pass me, and so I played the waiting game.

I sat on the couch for half an hour, drank two beers, and now played pool by myself, hitting balls back and forth. The living room was vacant because everyone else was sent away for the day for various missions or was patrolling around the compounds, which I was scheduled to be taking someone else's duty in an hour, so the commander needed to leave.

Footsteps were heard off in the distance, and I began to sweat as they got closer. Trying to keep my mind occupied, I continued to hit the balls but occasionally looked up from the table. He appeared and walked past me. As he was going to exit, he turned around, looked at me, and then said, "Come join me after dinner. I have something for you."

"Sure thing."

He then walked out the door. I watched him as he walked past the large deck and down the stairs. He turned the corner and then disappeared. I took a deep breath and placed the pool stick on the table, grabbed my beer, and made my way to his office.

As I looked around the corner, I found the corridor empty. I made my way to his office. The corridor was longer, colder, and darker on this day that I performed the act that was illegal and punishable in the eyes and laws of the compound.

I had second thoughts about doing this but eventually entered. I sat behind his desk and opened each door, rummaging through the various papers and pens. In the bottom drawer, I saw a safe key. I grabbed it and then turned to see the safe just sitting on the floor. The safe soon opened as I peered inside and saw jewelry that had been stolen and several stacks of money. I didn't want to take out too much in case he came later to look at the possessions. I grabbed a handful of cash, enough to find transportation and food for the next few days until we could find a safe place to stay.

Once finished, I closed the safe and returned the key to the cluttered drawer, closed it, and rushed out of the room, stuffing the money in my pocket.

I rushed down the corridor, into the living room, and out the front door. My feet pounded, my palms were sweaty, and I knew that after stealing the money, there was no turning back. Either I escape, or I die. When he finds out money is missing, he will search the entire compound. If anyone is found with the cash, the commander will shoot him on the spot.

***

That night, after dinner, anxiety filled my body. I sat on a chair with my arms folded, raising them to scratch and touch my face. My eyes searched the communal room, and my stomach churned at the imminent escape. I counted the minutes and hours until the escape would happen. Images of being caught and beaten—even killed—filled my thoughts throughout the day. I didn't know what would happen, but I dreaded the image that cast in my distant memory.

The commander was sitting on the deck. He looked as if he knew nothing of my plan, which eased my tension. I approached him and stood there until he waved me to come forward. He pointed to the seat, which I took, hoping and praying that he didn't look too close at the contents in his safe.

"Aderito, I just wanted to see you. I haven't had the pleasure of your company in quite some time."

I nodded in agreement, as the commander looked over at the young woman who was standing in the dark corner. He snapped his fingers, and she nodded and left. She returned a few minutes later with a silver tray. On the tray, there was a pile of white flaky substance. It was cocaine. On the tray, there was a single-dollar bill and a single blade of a box cutter knife.

The tray was placed in the middle of the table.

"Please, help yourself."

I paused and looked at the substance. I didn't pause because I didn't know what to do with it; in fact, I knew how to sniff it. I didn't pause because I didn't want it. In fact, I was craving the feeling that it caused. I paused because I knew that it might flatten me for the night and then escaping could be near impossible. However, denying the gesture would mean punishment. Maybe I could take one snort and then act tired and excuse myself.

Reaching for the money, I rolled it in the tube, grabbed the box cutter knife, and moved a small amount toward me so that it separated from the rest of the pile. I hit the blade several times back and forth, moving it into a straight line. Once it was perfect, I placed the money in my right nostril. I closed the other with my free hand, started from one end, and moved to the other, snorting the entire substance. The hit sent an immediate chill through my body. My head went back, and my body shivered from the feeling. A small amount of cocaine remained on my nose. I wiped it off with one finger, licked it clean, and handed the money to the commander, who proceeded to do the same.

I watched as he went through the same ritual. Once he was done, I knew that I had to escape the conversation. I yawned and raised my hands in the air so that he was sure to see that I was tired.

"You know, the other soldiers are not happy with your protection of that girl."

I stopped yawning. "Oh, really? Why?"

"I don't know, but it's best that she is freed so that other men can enjoy her company."

"But she has a baby."

"I don't want to hear any more of it. I have made my decision," he said with a wide smile, stretching his arms out as if he were going to hug me. "Now come. Continue. Let's get wild and high." He stretched his arms wider and laughed in the air.

"I must be going. I am awfully tired."

He moved forward and then slammed his fists on the table, forcing the cocaine to jump. "This is a gift. Are you going to shove this gift back into my face?" He lowered his eyebrows and shoulders and moved in my direction with his fists clenched tight.

"No, of course not," I stammered to an answer.

"Good, then let's continue."

We took one sniff after the other, and the pile was getting smaller. My head was starting to get light. The opened dining room patio was spinning. The sensation and images that were in my mind made of strange people who morphed in different shapes. My eyes were spinning. I looked up at the lights that strung above, and then my head landed hard in the middle of the smaller pile of cocaine; and then I was out, in the physical presence, but my mind and body were conscious, feeling the presence of others and hearing muffled sounds.

The commander pointed to me. Two strong men came over and hoisted me in the air. One grabbed me by the hands and the other by the feet. They carried me across the walkway and threw me on the bed. I lay as if I were dead. Cocaine lingered just above my lip and on my cheek. Every time I breathed, more went in my nose. I licked my lips and felt the sweet taste of heaven.

My roommates soon entered and retired for the evening. They laughed as they saw my hands dangling by the side of the bed. I still wore my boots, and my breathing was slow and steady. I didn't move, but I sensed the room spinning but my body in full sedation and relaxation.

Soon, the rest of the compound retired until the only sounds were the violin of the crickets playing their music. The wind was still, and the earth lit up by the high stars and the half moon.

***

"Hoot, hoot," Victoria made the owl sound. She paced back and forth outside my room. Victoria continued to make the sound, but I didn't come. She looked frantic around the deadly silent and empty compound. Victoria opened the door and peeked around the corner. The other people sleeping in my room didn't move. She walked over to where I lay and shook my shoulders, but there was no response. Victoria saw the cocaine on my cheek and hit the bed out of anger.

She lowered her head to my ear and said, "Sorry, but I must leave."

Victoria looked under my bed and rummaged through my piece of luggage where I kept my clothes and other small possessions. She found nothing as she looked for the money. Victoria looked around and finally at my pockets. She reached in the first pocket and found nothing. Victoria reached across, nearly lying on top. She lowered her hand inside my pocket, felt the wad of cash, and grabbed it, transferring it to her pocket.

Victoria looked around once more and saw the gun propped against the wall. She grabbed it, then went over to me once more, kissed me on the forehead, and then walked out the door.

The baby tied to her back cried as she ran away from my room, around the corner, and disappeared into the night.

CHAPTER 23

A pounding on my door brought my soul back to life. My head hurt, and I felt like I had died many times last night, only to come back to life and live another day. I sat up on my bed and landed my feet on the cement floor. I rubbed my eyes, trying to get my sight back. The man knocked on the door again. I rubbed my eyes back and forth, and my head flinched from side to side. My body posture collapsed as I tried to gather my strength to stand and go toward the continuous pounding, which sent further pain through my head.

Confused and trying to figure out why someone might be frantically knocking repeatedly clouded my judgment. Then the image of Victoria popped into my head, and I remember her coming into my room and talking with the lifeless body, but I couldn't remember much more. Had she tried to escape? Had she made it? Does the man at the door want to alert me? The questions put a spark in my step as I jumped to my feet and raced toward the door. I opened and saw a young man decked out in his military attire standing there, holding his AK-47. .

"The commander wants you by the tree."

The man walked away as I tried to ask him why, but before I gathered my words, he was around the corner. Dressed with my boots and everything, I ran out the door and around the corner. I walked a few hundred feet, turned another corner, and my heart dropped as I wanted to die.

Two soldiers held Victoria by the arm, and the commander punched her several times. Victoria's head and arms lay limply, and a constant stream of blood came from her mouth. Her chest thrust out and then retreated as she tried to gather strength, but she had none left. Victoria's face bruised, and both eyes bulged out of the socket and formed a dark deep red ring that appeared to be spreading.

Her baby sat on the ground behind her, crying.

The commander grabbed her hair, lifted her head, and looked at his work. His eyes were intent on examining every inch of her face. His eyes were cold and dark, and anger boiled. The commander thought she was worthless and should be scorned for her behavior. I saw him mouth the word *bitch* and then slap her face once more. As the hard blow landed on her beaten body, his veins bulged and twitched; and he breathed heavily, causing his lips to rattle.

The commander circled her slowly. Her breathing increased; her crying and pleading grew louder. The commander stopped in front. He lifted his boot and then kicked hard in her rib cage. Her ribs cracked, and the screaming pursued as she flew backward and slid to a stop in front of her crying baby. She looked up at the child, and her eyes filled with sorrow. Her stare was empty and distant as she tried in a failed attempt to reach her child. Her chin trembled, and tears rolled out of her eyes as her body shook toward the baby, knowing that what she was doing would be useless.

The two men came and grabbed her by the shoulders. She resisted being hoisted. I think she wanted to look deep into her baby's brown eyes as she sensed that might be the last time she was able to do so.

"No," she screamed as her outstretched hands tried to grab ahold of the baby. Every ounce of energy she had went into her last struggle toward her creation, who now wailed and flew his little arms to be helped by his mother.

It was to no avail as the men placed her back on her knees.

The commander looked into the crowd of onlookers and spotted me in the middle, trying to show little emotion, but my mind and body were racing with worry.

"Aderito, come here, my boy."

I stepped forward. I wondered if he knew what the plan was and that I was to go with her.

"Do you know what this bitch did?"

I shook my head no, hoping he didn't just catch me in a lie.

"One of the guards last night caught her trying to escape and found a wad of cash," he said, pulling out money I had stolen. "My money," his voice raised as he directed the words toward where she shook.

He placed the money back in his pocket. "The bitch must be punished, and you are going to do the punishing . . . after all, she is your bitch, and you didn't keep a close eye on her."

He paused, looking into my face, and saw absolute terror because I didn't know how I was going to punish her. The commander looked toward the crowd and shouted, "Aderito will punish this girl. I sentence her to death."

He said this, hoping to get a cheer and a reaction from the crowd, but he got nothing. When he said the word *death*, my mouth went dry. A tear rolled down my cheek. I wanted to hide my emotion in front of the commander, but I couldn't. My hands shook. She looked up at me, and I shook my head. I told myself not to do it. How could I kill the lifeline, the woman who kept me going and gave me hope? How was I going to kill her, execution style? I loved her too much.

She and I stared at each other. Her face bloodied and beaten, my eyes and mouth dropped, and eyes filled with tears.

The commander came toward me and handed me a pistol that he carried in his pocket. My shaking hand reached for it and held it tight. I walked toward her. As I walked, I thought of everything that might convince the commander to spare her life. I thought of turning the gun on the commander, but then everyone would kill me and then Victoria, and I would have accomplished nothing.

I approached her until I was only a few feet away and held the gun to her head. My hands were shaking; more tears filled my eyes, and I couldn't see straight.

I looked around at the commander and said in one last effort to save her life, "I think she has learned a lesson. Can't we tie her to the tree like you did for me?"

"You were a good soldier. I didn't want to lose you. She is expendable. Now shoot the bitch, or you can join her."

My chest was aching, and my arms became weak. The world spun in a continuous downward spiral. My throat and mouth ached, and words could not be released. I sniffed and wiped my nose clean. My face vibrated, and I wailed out a loud cry, unable to eliminate the pain.

I raised the gun back to her head. I was so scared; my hand couldn't keep the gun straight. My knees were quaking, and my heart was pounding. I wanted to cry and scream at the barbaric act, yet I was a coward that said nothing and made no stance toward the greater justice. The only thing left to do was to kill her. I grabbed the trigger, and then the sounds of her baby crying filled the air. What would happen to the baby? I released my grip on the trigger and looked at her child.

My breathing became deeper. I wiped away my tears, which soaked my skin. Now sweat consumed my body. Victoria looked up at me. Fear was in her eyes. She was a weakened woman, with barely enough strength to open her swollen eye and stare at me. Her soul was dead, and it had been for a long time. She had lived in hell, seen it for far too many years, and I sensed she was ready to die.

"Do it. Save my life from this hell."

I cried more, and my mouth opened, wanting to say something; but no words were found, just weeping sounds. I wiped away my tears, dropped hard to my knees, and crawled to her, holding her head and hugging her body.

"I am so sorry," I managed to say in a weeping voice.

"Take care of my baby," she quivered to a response.

I held the gun toward her head and looked into her eyes. I watched as her body shook, and tears consumed her cheeks. She closed her eyes, and I did the same. I placed my finger on the trigger—and pulled it. The bullet pierced through her brain, and she stopped beating life. The men holding her arms let go, and her limp body fell into mine. I dropped the gun and held her close, rocking back and forth. I lowered my head into her bloodied face. My tears flowed as I cried loudly for the entire group to see because I didn't care that they were looking at me, so I kept crying, and I couldn't stop.

I hated the monster inside of me, feeling that I was weak and not able to protect her.

The commander came behind me and picked up the gun. "I can't have a bastard baby in my compound," he said with intense emotion.

He walked over to the baby and without hesitation pulled the trigger. The sound of the bullet shook the ground. The baby's weakened skull, crushed from the impact of the bullet in his head, made him unrecognizable. I screamed louder as I looked at the baby lying there. I continued to scream, and once I started, I couldn't stop. Tears filled my eyes, and the shock of the deaths left my ears and sight in shambles. I heard nothing around me. I saw nothing and felt only the rapid beat of my heart and the lifeless pulse of Victoria wrapped in my own fear.

The crowd left; and now Victoria, the baby, and I lay in the field. I crawled over to the baby and lifted him. I held him firmly against my chest and crawled back over to his mom, placing the baby on top of Victoria, and the two of them on my lap.

I pretended that they were still alive, but the reality continued to haunt me as I looked at the bullet holes in each of their heads. Blood continued to flow from their bodies, soaking me and forcing us to sit in the pool of mixed blood. I continued to sit there with my legs tucked under my body, and I couldn't leave.

Victoria's head rested on the ground as I wrapped her hands around the baby and then I lay next to them. I wrapped my hands around Victoria's waist and rested my head gently on her shoulders, giving her a kiss on her neck. I wept in and out in a shaking tone. My hands and body now covered in her blood, yet none of this mattered.

I lay with the bodies most of the day but couldn't force myself to say good-bye. I cried until I was too tired to cry anymore. Once the sun started to set, I hoisted the bodies into my arms. The baby lay on top, and Victoria's limbs dangled to the ground and a shovel placed near my chest. They were heavy, but the emotions and anger allowed me to carry them with ease. I took the bodies over to the far end of the compound where they would rest for eternity.

I placed the two on the ground, took the shovel, dug, and continued to dig until there was a hole three feet deep. My bloodied clothes now had a second layer of dirt plastered. I placed them in the ground and poured the dirt over their bodies, for them to rest peacefully.

I stood by the raised mound. I looked deep into the ground and pondered the memories, the destruction and emotion that we had together. Thinking of her lying with her baby brought more tears back. I fell to my knees, and then my body went limp on the ground; and I rested, tired and emotional, next to the grave.

I couldn't help but think that such a magnificent woman and full of spirit was buried so unceremoniously. No one was around to honor her, remember her, and celebrate her life and existence on the cruel world. No one was coming to burry a traitor and a thief. I saw her as a wonderful mother, the spirit that was unshaken, even in the darkest hours. She was a wonderful person, whom I loved.

Later, I walked back to my bed, drained, and realized that I might have taken her life but she was set free from the life she hated and now rested with the angels, where she is at peace. I gained comfort thinking of this.

CHAPTER 24

I sulked around the compound for the last few days. Every time I went to sleep, I thought of Victoria and the way she made me feel. I then thought of the night that she tried to escape and what might be different if I wasn't so high and escaped with her. We might have made it and could be far away from this place, happy and running. The images were eating me inside.

I didn't talk with anyone. They knew my anger, and people couldn't break through the hard shell that I put around me, which shielded my emotion from the rest of the world.

I didn't know how to survive or escape. Deep down, I knew that I needed to honor her life, which meant escaping, but the thought seemed impossible. Every time I thought of a plan, I realized that dying in any insane manner would not be honoring her life. The only choice was to live, even though at times I wanted to take my own life.

The whole compound was loading guns and ammunition into the trucks. I didn't know what it was for, but we were leaving just before the sun started to set. We were planning to be at our final destination when it got darker. Whatever the plan, it must be a momentous one because most of the compound was directed to go.

I helped load AK-47s and ammunition. As I loaded the weapons, a pit in my stomach lingered because I didn't know how to kill another person. At the same time, if I didn't, they would kill me. The commander said it himself that I was an exemplary soldier, and that is why he spared my life and Victoria's wasn't. What might happen if I became expendable? I have come to know that once a soldier becomes a liability, he is discarded as if a rotten piece of meat. The soldiers cost money. He needs to feed them and house them, and if they aren't living up to the expectations set by the commander, he would just as soon kill them as pay for them to eat.

We waited for the commander to give orders to load the truck and head out. I sat in the first truck, bare chested with a black tank top draped over my right shoulder. My hands placed on my knees and clasped together, and my gun leaned against my left leg.

I waited for the commander to sit in the front seat of one of the vehicles that went on the journey, but he didn't. He stood as if he were a coward. He wouldn't dare go out and fight; he just assumed striking fear in us to do his killing. The only killing he did was in the comfort of the compound, surrounded by his own men. He was a fucking coward, whom I grew to hate.

Calisto sat next to me. He had gotten taller and had become immensely brave. Calisto turned out to be an obedient little soldier, who reminded me of myself a few years ago. He wasn't cynical or had grown to hate the place or the people he called his family. Calisto still had a wish to prove his manhood, and he still wanted to be loved by the commander. Someday, if he survived, he will realize that the commander gave nothing but fake affection.

He sat on the flooring of the truck while I sat on the wall. We soon were off, and I found myself in a familiar place, sitting in the truck with the wind blowing and hanging on as we went through every bump in the road. My mind was always racing about the upcoming kill. I sat in these moments in deep thought, as if I were on the acclaimed African hunting safari, trying to kill the mighty lion or the gigantic elephant. I wished that was where I was going, but I always knew that the kill I was after was another human.

As the convoy of trucks journeyed the dirt road, the sun set behind the horizon; and now we sat in darkness, with the subtle glow of the headlights to light up our faces.

I looked to Calisto, who was shivering. He wasn't shivering because of terror or thoughts of the kill; he was cold because of the gentle breeze blowing through the truck.

I touched his back and gave him a smile. He smiled back. He and I didn't see each other much, but I was always connected with him, and he admired me for what I had done on the dreadful battles.

Maybe this might be my new friend. The new person who could take Victoria's place and help me survive.

"Are you ready?" I said, trying to make small talk, unsure of what I should say to ease the tension.

"Yeah, I am always ready. You know where we are going?"

"No, sorry, but it's probably some small village that we are going to take control of."

He nodded in agreement, rested his hand on the bed of the truck, and leaned his body over the side, watching the ground whiz past. Calisto then looked ahead of the truck but only saw as far as the headlights; the rest was dark.

We sat the rest of the hour in silence. The only sounds heard was the gale rushing through our faces, the trucks roaring around the dirt, and chirping of the various insects that came out at night. For a moment, I was at peace. I forgot the troubles that I faced, and there was a weight lifted from my shoulders. The sounds that surrounded me, the cool breeze, which kept me calm, felt peaceful.

I took in deep breaths through the smogless sky. I consumed my thoughts on the stars, which appeared bright, sitting over our heads. It appeared to be the perfect night, but this ended as we pulled into a small village, which, by appearances from the outside, looked abandoned.

I couldn't help but stare at the building in the center of the town and houses that surrounded them. They looked familiar as if I had seen them in a past life. My mind flooded with images, but I couldn't place the sights that I was looking at with an image of my past life.

"What is this place called?" I shouted to a soldier who stood up in front of the truck, looking powerful.

"Homoine," the soldier answered.

The name sounded familiar, but I had forgotten this place. I had forgotten where I came from, what this place meant to me. It was a distant memory, one that I didn't know if I would get back.

The convoy of vehicles stopped in front of the hospital, with the bright Red Cross that hovered at the top of the building. The hospital looked familiar. I had glimpses of this image in my mind but found no recollection of being here. The soldiers got out of the vehicles and reached for weapons.

I stood frantically looking around. A group of soldiers spread out into the village while the rest walked into the hospital. A man was standing at the entrance. His hands were outstretched, trying to get us to stop.

"Please there are sick people here. Please don't harm us," the man said, dreaming that his begging and his hands stretched out toward us could stop the violence. The first soldier in line shot the man dead. We walked through the first pool of blood and continued our journey through the corridors, leaving bloody footprints.

"No one leaves here alive," a man shouted as the soldiers spread out in the hospital.

I walked down the darkened corridor and entered a room that housed sick children. Many parents sat by the bedside of their loved ones. The room was strangely familiar to me. I walked in, the room was lit by several dim lights, and one light in the corner flickered. More soldiers entered. One raised his weapon and shot several times in the air.

The patients and the loved ones screamed and covered their ears at the sounds of the gunshots piercing through the ceiling and knocking white debris to the floor. They shook as we walked, looking at each victim. The one and only exit was guarded, so the children appeared trapped in a cage. They feared for their life. The fear, however, fueled our anger.

I walked to the far end of the room. There was this small child, about six years of age. She had lost her leg, which now had a tight bandage, covering the trace of the cut. Her body propped by her arms, and she looked into my dark eyes. She didn't look scared; she was content with my presence. I didn't understand. Most people would be afraid and hide their bodies from the sight of a child soldier.

I raised my gun and walked toward her. The gun was placed to her head. Her chest pounded, and sweat drenched her face, yet she did not flinch. She stood strong, and I had to admire that. But she had to die. The gun sounded in the small room, and she fell into her bed. The shot echoed for several seconds. Cries and screams filled the small space, and the rest of the soldiers followed my lead.

One by one, people shot by the soldiers. I moved to the next bed where a young boy hid under his blankets. I shot several times, and now his blanket soaked up the blood that gushed from his body.

A mother and her child sat, hugging each other. The mother's body shielded the child from the destruction that lurked within the sick bay. I didn't hesitate. I raised my weapon and shot seven times. Every bullet pierced through the mother's back and exited into the young child's stomach and chest. Both people fell to the floor—dead.

As if the thought of this morning had left my mind, I was now in a darker place, a place of the devil. I went from one bed to the next; everyone had to die. I took no mercy on anyone. Once they had met their end, we exited the room and continued through the corridor.

As I walked in long strides, the sounds and echoes of guns firing lingered in the cold night. Screams of victims or soon-to-be victims and images of them running as if they were a herd of antelope, trying to figure out how to escape yet knowing that death was just around the corner.

I exited the first building and now stood in a large compound where there were other isolated sick bays. Victims were running. I scanned the compound, and in each building, guns firing blasted and echoed off the walls. Each time the weapon fired, smoke escaped the aperture, and a subtle yellow glow lit up the silhouetted images of hands reaching for the sky and then falling to their deaths. I looked over in the distance and saw the maternity ward.

Three men walked in with guns and soon started to fire. Mothers-to-be and their babies killed one after another.

Time to work, I thought.

The first man who ran by, I aimed and let three bullets enter his body. None of the bullets killed the victim, but they all hit him. He lay in his own blood, covering his wounds, panting heavily. He saw me coming, to finish the kill, and he started to crawl away. I stood over his body as he made one last valiant effort to escape, but I placed my boot on his head and stopped him in his tracks. I lowered my knee on his back and held it there, firm. With the other knee, I pressed his head against the rocky ground. He winced in pain but said nothing. I reached into my belt, grabbed a sharp knife, leaned toward his hand, grabbed his wrist, and pulled it toward me. I pressed the knife against his skin and started to cut. The man was able to find his voice, and he moved around wiggling, trying to get me off, but I trapped him. He kicked his feet, high into the air, but it was useless. I continued to cut his arm at the elbow joint and cut through the flesh before reaching the bone. I continued to cut through the tendons and joints, ignoring his screams and cries. Finally, his arm was severed, and I threw it in front of his eyes so that he could see. The remains of his arm moved around vigorously. Blood squirted out of the vein of this jagged-cut limb. I lifted my legs off his body and now straddled the man once more. He cried loud and tried to leave, but without irresolution, I let two more bullets enter his brain.

I spent no time contemplating the murder. The next victim was shot dead. One after the other, people fell to their knees and now lay in their blood. It was like target practice or a game, which I was winning.

"Aderito," a voice said wobbly.

I turned around, but it wasn't a brother. I looked into his eyes, and I saw my own. Who was the man who knew my name? I stepped closer, and he stepped into the light. I knew him but couldn't remember. It looked like someone from my past, whom I had forgotten. I stood, scared and trembling in a deep thought. The sounds of the guns and the screaming men and women falling to their deaths became silent. Nothing was seen or heard, but I fixated my energy and attention on the man who stood before me with outstretched hands, wanting a hug.

I didn't run to him, which scared the man for some reason. My mind raced back and forth, and I remembered nothing.

The bullet hit the ground a few feet from where I stood. This shook me out of the trance. I heard the screams and the sounds of war once more. I ran to the man with my gun pointed straight at him and yelled in the air as a battle cry. I reached toward him, pushed repeatedly until I reached a gigantic rock, and pushed the large man over and watched him tumble to his back. He now lay, with his arms still reaching toward me.

I stood on the rock and jumped, high in the air, and landed on his chest, pinning the man to the ground. I sat, placing my weight on his body. I threw my AK-47 aside and grabbed my handgun, which was placed in the holster, attached to my belt. Pulling my gun out, I pointed at his face, but I hesitated. For a reason unbeknownst to me, I couldn't bring myself to kill him.

The man, much larger than me, could have seized the opportunity and thrown me off, grabbed my AK, and shot me dead—but he didn't. He lay there, gazing into my eyes, seeing his own reflection.

"It's me, your father, Amani," the man said, trying to explain. "Do you not remember me, your own blood?"

Fear struck the man. He didn't know what to do as he lay there trembling at what I have become.

Father—I couldn't remember a father. The father I knew was at the compound. Images of that father rushed through my mind. The only images that I contemplated were the beatings, forcing me to kill Victoria, and then the commander turning the gun on the baby. What father was he? Did he love me? Could this be the father that was in a distant memory?

I hit my head, trying to remember the man who lay before me. Fuzzy images started to enter my thoughts. As I thought harder, the images became clearer; and the man who stood before reentered, and I remembered happier times.

I got off the man, dropped my weapon, and propped myself up against the rock. I started to cry. The rock-solid soldier that was created broke down like a child, the man remembered. The man, my father, got to his knees and rushed to my side. He hugged me hard into his hands and cried on my shoulders, holding me for an eternity. My father kissed my forehead, which was a loving embrace that I longed for, the one that the commander never gave. I wept harder into my father's arms as more images flooded my mind, and I knew I was home.

"My child, you must be strong. Meet me out front, and I will take you home and protect you. Your mother and I have been looking for you for a long time."

Mother! I remembered the family I wanted to find. Images of my mother chasing after the truck that changed my life flooded my thoughts, which made me sad. I couldn't wait to embrace her once more.

My father rose to his feet and started to run into the building, through the corridor, and outside, in front, where he waited.

I grabbed my weapons and started following. A soldier who had watched me let my father go walked up behind me and grabbed my hand. He held me tight, and his eyes glared. The soldier reached for his gun and was going to shoot, but I raised my weapon first and shot him several times in the neck and chest. He fell to his knees and then toppled to the ground. I looked around to make sure that no one else saw the incident.

I grimaced at the man next to my feet. My body was overheating, and my stomach fluttered as I stared at the dead man whom, just a few minutes ago, I called my brother. I was confused at the thought of killing him and running toward an immemorial memory.

I started to run through the corridor and outside where my father stood. He held out his hand and grabbed mine, and we started to run.

The sounds of gunfire surrounded us. Screams and fire blazing from the burning houses shot fear. Each step I took through the soft sand and debris that had fallen from the trees brought more memories back. Each step, I got closer to my freedom. My eyes scanned the horizon, trying to avoid soldiers that could cause a disruption to my escape.

We approached a familiar house. The bathroom and latrine looked similar to an image I once had; the tree that stood strong in the middle was still standing, and the house that I once dreaded was now a beautiful sight.

My father ran to the front door and pounded hard. There was no response.

"Michelle, it's me. Open the door," he said, calling for my mother to open.

The door opened, and we entered the living room. My father locked the door behind, and I stared into my mother's eyes. It took me several minutes to gather my thoughts and formulate the images of her, but she recognized me instantly. Water filled her eyes, and her lips shook as she walked closer. She hugged me hard and rubbed her hands around my back. I wrapped my hands around her, and we began to weep.

"I am so happy. You have come back to me," she said, kissing my head.

"Quickly, we must go to Aderito's bedroom . . . and hide."

My father turned off the lights and ushered us to my bedroom. I walked in and could see nothing, but it smelled just as I remembered. We sat on the cold floor away from the casements. I sat in the middle, and my mother and father, who could not believe their eyes, hugged me and rocked me back and forth, as if I were ten years old again. I didn't complain as this felt right and warm.

The guns continued to ring throughout the village. Screams continued to echo through my room, and the three of us fell asleep, listening to each other's hard breaths and the sounds of gunfire and smells of burning houses and flesh that consumed the air.

CHAPTER 25

I woke up on the floor. My eyes scanned the room, and I covered my face from the sun shining in my eyes. I sat up and leaned against the bed in the corner, rubbing my eyes, trying to gain a sense of normalcy. Voices in the distance were heard but could not be made out whom they came from or what they were saying.

My eyes were bloodshot, my hands were shaking, and my whole body was shivering. There was a desire and need to have a fix. I needed cocaine. For as long as I could remember, I was given a hit as a gift or reward for the good deeds. I was like a dog after performing a trick and needed the reward, or I became depressed and longed for the sensation that the drugs created.

I crawled around the room, pushed things to the side, and opened the suitcases as I tried to find what I longed for, but could see nothing.

My parents rushed into the room and found me in the corner, shaking back and forth. They rushed to my side and rubbed me on the leg. They lifted me to my feet and walked me over to the bed. My mother wrapped my body in a blanket and gave me a gentle side hug.

"What's the matter?" my father asked.

"I need it. I want it so that I can calm down."

"What do you need?" my mother said, rubbing my back.

"Heroine," I said, not wanting to hide it.

My mother gulped and looked at my father and then said, "We don't have any . . . you can't have any."

"Jesus . . . what did they do to you?" my father said.

"Let me go make you some tea and breakfast." My mother rushed out of the room.

My father followed. I climbed further onto the bed, curled my knees near my chest, and continued to rock back and forth, sweating.

***

I sat in my room for a long time before getting up to pace. I had not taken a bath, and my room started to smell as foul as a dead cat.

My parents kept talking outside my room. It was about me, but I couldn't make out the faint whisper. My mom came in to see me but soon left when she saw me sleeping, sweating, and smelling strongly my filth hit her.

On the second day, I woke up with a headache and depressed from my constant pain. However, today was better than most. I walked out of my bedroom and into the living room where my parents sat. They rose from the couch and greeted me, surprised from my presence from a near-dead state.

I took a bucket bath that day and felt much better. Once the shower finished, I went back inside, got dressed, and sat on a chair across from where my parents sat. We didn't know what to say, so we sat there in quietude for a while.

I broke down and started to cry. My mom rushed over to where I sat and put her arms around me. I cried into them for a while before I told them my story. I told them about the drugs, the drinking, and the killing. When I wanted to tell them about Victoria and killing her, I cried so hard that I couldn't utter the words.

Once I started sharing my story, I couldn't stop. It was wonderful to get the issues out on the table, and I felt that I had an audience of people to whom I could talk to and not fear being killed.

"I am so sorry for everything," I said, crying into my own hands.

I looked up at my dad and mom, who both had tears on their cheeks.

"You have nothing to be sorry about." My dad leaned forward and placed his hand on my knees.

"They forced you to do these things, and somewhere inside, that same boy who left us . . . is in there," my mother said, pointing toward my chest.

"You aren't mad?" I said, quivering.

"Of course not. We are just happy that you have come back to our home."

My mom hugged me in her arms, and I was delighted to know that someone loved me and accepted me even with the terrible things that I had done. We cried and hugged each other and shared other stories for the next few hours before I went back into my bedroom and went to sleep in the midst of the day.

CHAPTER 26

Over 380 bodies were dragged and placed in rows in front of the hospital, a grim reminder of the deadly day in July. A day in which I traveled home with people I once called brothers and took fire against innocents for nothing more than a political point. My body ached and sickened by the sight of the bodies being prepared for burial. Lifeless corpses lay limp, exposed to the harsh weather and decomposing by the second, leaving a stench in the air.

Young boys looked brave as they carried the last few bodies and placed them in front of the hospital to be transported and buried. The young men covered in sweat stains lowered their heads and appeared somber as they tried to perform their duty, from the place of death to the pile of corpses. The sweat eliminated the small tears that formed as they were unable to hide the bravery of their deeds.

I felt guilty, looking at these bodies. I wanted to go over and say sorry to the living, but would they understand or would they kill me? Ultimately, I couldn't ponder the words, because if I were in their situation, I would have killed myself. My mother had lost me once, and I couldn't allow her to lose me a second time.

I walked around the dead bodies. I have seen too many who lost their lives too young. You might think that I was used to it, but this time was different. There was a desire and need to kill before, but now that I was safe from enemies who lurked a few miles away, I felt complete sorrow.

As I walked around, I covered my mouth and nose with the sleeve of my long shirt, which my mother had purchased the day before because most of my clothes didn't fit from when I was younger. The smell was horrible. It had been four full days since the killings, and the town had been preparing for the mass burial the entire time. Bodies had been lying in the hot sun, decomposing every minute; and as a result, maggots and flies covered the outside and worked their way to the inside. The smell was unbearable, and I felt like running away, but I needed to see my destruction to move on, so I paid special attention to look at every body to ensure that I paid my respects.

I stopped in front of a young girl. It took me a second to recall who she was. Her body was covered with flies, maggots, and she smelled like a rotten carcass. The young girl was brave and fearless toward the enemy. She was the young girl I had killed regardless of the respect I felt for her. Now she lay here, piled on top of several other bodies, eyes closed with a bullet through the head and flesh rotting in the hot sun. I could bear the sight no more and ran away from the bodies behind the wall of the hospital, lowered my head, and placed my hands on my knee, with my backside against the wall. I opened my mouth and let my modest breakfast come up on the ground. The smell and taste of the vomit coming up made my stomach sick.

As I spit the last pieces out of my mouth, a truck backed up to the bodies. I looked around the corner and saw young men grabbing them by the hands and feet and throwing them in the back of the truck. It was strange, and I felt mad at their careless behavior. Just a few days ago, I disrespected people so much that I killed them and felt satisfied at the destruction that I caused. I felt like a man, watching older people beg for their life. It was a sickness that I couldn't get rid of, and now my stance was the opposite, and what I felt was remorse. I was angry with the dead bodies lying so unceremoniously and tossed around as if their lives meant nothing on this planet.

The emotions that were running through my body couldn't be explained. I was going through withdrawal, not having my daily fix of heroin every time I woke up. When I slept, images flashed through my head that brought the past, crashing me back into reality. Images of Victoria being shot, the old man begging for his life before being killed, and men, women, and children dying because of my actions. Everything I saw or remembered made me cry. It felt as if I couldn't stop. I once tried not showing emotions or crying out of fear of the ramifications of my actions. Now I couldn't stop, even when comforted.

I couldn't bear the bodies or the transportation of the corpses that would be buried in a mass grave, so I began to walk away from the hospital to clear my head.

I found my way back to the river. There was no one there. Not a single kid running and playing or a woman cleaning her clothes. I sat on the bank, with my feet soaking by the gentle-moving water. The zephyr whistling in my ear and the smell of the refreshing breeze made me feel at peace. A smile broke free.

As I looked at the river, memories of Victoria playing and jumping in the water, of seeing her the first time, and of her kissing me on the lips came flooding into my mind. I remembered her innocence, which is what I loved.

A lump in my throat formed, but I did not cry. I continued to smile as the sights and the memories flooded my thoughts, and I remembered the safety and tranquility. I wanted for Victoria to be sitting next to me and for me to look into her eyes, push her in the water, and run in the hard dirt.

Lowering my head, I closed my eyes and wished that when they opened, she sat beside me. I am not sure if it was magic, a ghost, or a wishful thought; but when I opened my eyes and looked to my right, she sat there. Her hair puffed up and blew in the breeze. She had a large smile, her skin was free of bruises, and her eyes had no darkness. She was innocent again.

I smiled as I stared into her eyes and saw nothing but happiness. I hoped that this was her spirit, telling me that she was happy and received by the angels. She touched my back, and I felt shivers as goose bumps formed.

"I'm okay. I have been set free," she said in a rhythmic voice, as if she were singing from the heavens.

As we stood up, a subtle glow illuminated around her body. She was more beautiful and peaceful than I ever remembered. Her pure, innocent figure showed nothing but love and curiosity. The gentleness of her touch brought nostalgia into my thoughts, and everything appeared to be right.

She reached toward me and pushed my shoulder. She started to run around, and I followed suit, chasing after her. I lunged toward her body; but she ducked, lowering toward the ground, and then started to chase after me as I ran quickly into the water and felt her presence lurking behind, laughing as she tried to reach my shirt but was always a few inches short.

The laughter was innocent, and I could have listened to it for hours. As we ran, I felt her kick my heel, forcing me to fall to the ground and skid to a stop a few feet later. I turned around and saw her leap into the air, ready to land on my upper body. I could have moved, but I was mesmerized as her hair flipped into the air, and her glowing body spread out, ready to pounce. She landed on top of me, smiling as she grabbed my wrists and held them against the ground. My stomach rose and fell, and we shared a brief laugh as her hair engulfed my face. The hair smelled of roses, and her scarless skin felt beautiful.

We got up, and she grabbed my hands, clasping them and swaying back and forth. She pulled me near her, wrapped her arms around my neck, and rested her head on my shoulder. I grabbed her waist, and we began to dance in circles. We were light on our feet as we danced around the hard dirt, near the bank of the river. The music could not be heard, but the feeling of her close by in happier times was better than any sweet sound that may have rung down from the heavens.

We twirled around, deep in our own thoughts. My eyes remained closed, not wanting to open them and find her gone from life. The simple motion of twirling around, creating a blow of the breeze, lasted a few minutes; but sounds of her laughing, the dirt swooshing around, and the river flowing near our feet felt like a mesmerizing dream. I feared that the moment might pass, and I would be, once more, without her by my side.

I heard a loud laughter off in the distance, different from Victoria's. A young child of five years old ran from the trailhead and entered the water. He had not noticed that I was there, but the laughter forced my attention away from Victoria. When I tried to go back into the moment, I realized that I stood by myself, with my arms wrapped around the air; and once again, she was gone, out of my life.

I wasn't sure if what I had was real or just my imagination, but I was glad that we had one more moment together. That moment lingered with me for the rest of my life because it gave me comfort, knowing or believing that God had accepted her, even with her sins. I enjoyed the satisfaction that she was happy in her new home.

I walked past the child who now played in the river next to his mom washing clothes. I gave them a smile and walked up the hill and back into the village where they had finished loading the bodies in the truck, ready to take them to their final resting place.

CHAPTER 27

The bodies were buried early in the day. I elected to stay home, as I didn't want to see them anymore because of my emotional state. My mother and father went to the burial and were just returning, dressed in black attire.

They found me lying on the couch, staring at a blank TV. I was wrapped in a blanket, even though it was almost eighty-five degrees. My body was chilled and shaking. I was withdrawn today and was content in my complete isolation from the outside world. I felt a deep guilt of the past crimes and sadness of the events during the last week. The withdrawals from heroin were not helping with my depression as I couldn't leave the house. I didn't feel like showering or dressing, and I was content to spend the whole day staring into a blank TV, deep in my own thoughts and anxieties. I found that some days might be calm, like yesterday; and other times, I wanted to shoot myself, which was a strong qualm and desire to take my own life, almost as a punishment to rid the evil that still fought to come out and show its face to the world.

My mother walked over to me and gave me a kiss on my forehead, as she had been doing often since my return home. She then took a seat at the table, opposite of my father. She held her hands out toward his and waited for him to embrace her.

"I think we need to talk with the reverend about getting out of this country," my mother said firmly.

"Okay, you are right, but that will cost a lot of money. Do we have the cash?"

"I will get the cash from relatives in the States. We need out."

"What about Aderito's passport? Is it still valid?"

"Yes, it expires next year. Amani, I need out. It is too dangerous. I know that you wanted to come here to help your people, but it hasn't worked that way."

My mother caressed my father's hands gently, trying to soothe his needs. She smiled at him as he lowered his head and nodded in agreement. I think he realized the safety aspects of Mozambique and realized that it was time for the family to pack things up and leave.

"I'll talk with the reverend tomorrow, and we will make arrangements," my father stated as he rubbed my mother's hands.

***

The next day the reverend came to the house for lunch. We all sat around the table, talking about the exit and securing plane tickets and transportation to the airport in Maputo. I didn't say much. I was suffering from a headache, but the chills that I had yesterday seemed to dissipate.

As we sat at the table, we heard a truck rev the ugly engine in front of the house. We rose from the table and walked to the casement, where the curtains were still closed. We opened them just enough to see what was on the other side of the wall. My soul sank as I saw the commander with a few soldiers standing just in front to my home.

"That is the commander. They are probably coming back to find me," I said as I started to shake and pace back and forth, frantic at their presence. My eyes widened, and I couldn't find the strength to blink. I paced up and down the corridor, trying to escape from the threat, but realized that there was nowhere to go. The commander kept yelling from his truck, and I clasped my ears, trying to escape from the devilish sound. I shook my head vigorously as I leaned up against the wall and slid down, crouching toward the ground. I shook my head as I gasped for air. Thoughts continued to come to an outcome that would always leave me dead. My chest and lungs tightened at the thought.

The man driving kept honking his horn, and the commander kept yelling my name. Sweat started to form on my forehead. "Mom, I can't go back with them. Please don't make me go out there,"

I sobbed, shaking nervously. My lips and chin trembled as water formed in my eyes.

"No one is going to take you," my mom said as she leaned down, stopping me from moving around, holding me by the shoulders, and looking me in the eyes. "No one will take you," she repeated.

"You guys stay here. I will go talk with them," my father said as he walked toward the door.

My mother lunged toward him, grabbing him by the arm, and held him tight. She shook her head and then said, "Maybe they will go away. Maybe you don't have to leave."

"They obviously know that this used to be his home. They won't leave until they see someone. If I don't go now, they are liable to break into the house and kill us all. Just let me do this."

My mother's grip released, and my father turned the door handle. He took one last look at me and then left the house.

I got up from a crouched position and walked back toward the window. The curtain was opened at the bottom, allowing me to peek at the scene unfolding. I watched my father walk bravely toward the commander with his hands stretched out, signaling his wish for peaceful talks. He reached the commander, who was furious, biting his lips, expanding, and retracting his nostrils like an angry bull. I couldn't understand what he was saying, but his arms were flying wildly, and he kept pointing toward the house. My father would interrupt a few times. He clasped his hand as if he were asking for forgiveness, but I could tell that the commander was growing impatient.

The commander turned his back toward my father and then turned back around with his fists clenched tight together. With extreme force, his fist landed on my father's stomach. His body lunged forward. His mouth widened, and he gasped for his breath. The commander grabbed my father's chin and raised his head, then landed a hard left hook to his face. My father flew backward, and blood flew from his mouth. He landed on his knees with his face in the dirt and his buttocks sticking in the air.

I rushed toward the door, reaching for the handle, as the reverend grabbed my shoulder and threw me to the ground. Rising to my feet, I tried to rush toward the door again but was met by the reverend's massive embrace, holding me back, as I lunged forward. I moved violently around as I tried to free myself. More tears were cried, but the reverend would not let me go. Managing to free my hands, I placed them on his chest; and with all my strength, I pushed off from him, freeing myself, ready to take another run. My fist went back behind my head, and I contemplated hitting him when my mother stepped in front of me and held me back. My mom's embrace calmed me, and I stopped my struggle.

"I need to go. All they want is me," I cried.

"Your father would not want this," she yelled.

I stopped the fight but couldn't understand the reasons why I was being denied what I wanted. The thought of my father being beaten, bloodied and treated as a criminal was too much for me to handle; but I obliged my mother's wishes.

I went back to the casement. My father was on the ground. The commander came from behind and kicked him in the chest. My father rolled two times and landed on his back, looking up at the clear sky. The commander struck him again and then again, kicking four times in a row, and then sprawled over the body. The sun lit up his back and created a shadow over my father, and the sun glistened in the backdrop. He looked up at him, gasping for breath and weeping at the man who towered over.

The commander leaned down and was now a foot from his face. He asked him something. My father paused briefly and shook his head. The commander became enraged and punched him three times in the face. Blood splattered on the ground as the commander looked at his hand, which was now covered in my father's blood.

He looked over at a soldier and demanded a towel, which was promptly handed to him. The commander circled my father, wiping off the blood that painted his knuckles. He said nothing. He took pleasure watching him lie on the ground, holding his stomach, breathing heavily, and wincing from the sharp pain in his stomach and the cuts that covered his lower lip and nose.

My father turned to his side and placed his fist on the ground. He took two deep breaths, and out of a heroic act of defiance, he quickly lunged toward the commander. Dad wrapped his hands around his waist and pushed him hard against the tree. The commander's back cracked, and head flew back, slamming against the massive trunk. He grimaced in pain, and my father knew that soon the soldiers would come and stop him. He punched him in the stomach and then in the mouth. One punch after another landed on his face and then to his ribs and back to his face. My father was enraged, and once he got the first punch, he couldn't stop.

Soldiers came rushing over to my father. They grabbed him, and the commander fell to his knees and spit blood out of his mouth on to the ground. Black-and-blue bruises formed around his eyes, lips, and chin. Cuts gouged out around his mouth, and skin started to peel, forming large red gashes around the cheek.

The other soldiers surrounded my father. There were about five of them. They were so close to him that I couldn't even see him propped on his hands and knees. The soldiers started to beat him. One punch after the other landed on various spots on his body. My father fell to the ground, and the soldiers kicked him multiple times. His knees were close to his chest, and his hands covered his head. He flexed his body to try to take the blows, but the emotions and screams coming from the center circle indicated that his attempts at being a man were futile.

The commander got to his feet and walked over to his soldiers. He tapped them on the shoulders, and they stopped kicking my father and spread out to allow the commander to step forward.

My father turned on his back and looked up at the bloodied commander. However, my father was much worse. His entire face and mouth were covered from dripping blood, which now saturated his clothes. His face darkened, and eyes bulged out. He gasped and breathed heavily. The sun shining down on his face was too bright, and he closed his eyes.

The commander straddled my father, looked deep into his eyes, and wiped some of the blood from his mouth. His hands now bloodied again but this time with his own blood. While he was still straddling my father, he kneeled. One knee rested by my father's arm, causing agony, while the other knee was in the air. His left arm rested on his left leg, and his bloodied hand dangled by his side. He was talking to my father and saying something. He then spit on his face. My father winced as the wet substance, mixed with blood, splattered just around his eyes and cheeks. He then took the bloodied hand and wiped it on my father's forehead.

The commander got up from his knees and now once again stood over my father. I could tell that he wanted to stand, kick, and punch the commander again. He wanted to kill him, but he had no power to do so. The commander lifted his right foot and placed it on his mouth. He dug deep, pressing hard until he had pried open his mouth. He continued to dig into his mouth, stuffing his boot further down the throat. The commander bit his lip hard as he tried to put strength into his act of brutality.

He took the boot out, which now had bloodstains, and hovered it just above his mouth. He then came down hard, just to the right of his mouth; and my father's head went flying to the left, and the enormous splatter of blood spit out and flew toward the other soldier's boots. He let out a loud cry and spit out a tooth, and more blood trickled from his mouth. Dad panted harder and cried as he stared at the soldier's boots, hoping and praying for the pain to stop.

The commander snapped his fingers. Two soldiers picked up my father and propped him on his knees in front of the house, with his head looking at the window, where I still stood. The commander left briefly and went back to the truck. He grabbed a gas canister and walked over to my father.

He raised the canister over my father's head and began to pour. My father closed his mouth tight and closed his eyes. The entire canister emptied on my father, and now he sat covered with gas, wincing in pain and shaking at the thought of what might happen next.

The commander left once more and returned with a tire that was in the back of the truck. He placed the tire over my father's head and then pulled out a box of matches from his front pocket. As he held the matches over my father's head, the other soldiers gathered wood and placed it around my father. One soldier gathered another gas canister and soaked the wood and tire to allow maximum effects and to ensure that he would burn alive.

"Aderito, if you want your father to live, come out now," the commander yelled at the top of his lungs.

Once again, I tried to push my way through my mother to exit out of the room. My mother grabbed me by the shoulders, and the reverend helped. I fought, pushed, and almost punched both of them. I managed to push the reverend and my mother off and headed for the door. My mother gathered herself and lunged toward me, just as I reached out toward the knob. She managed to grab the waist of my blue jeans and, with one last effort, managed to pull me away from the door handle and push me back toward the corridor. The reverend locked the door and placed the key in his pocket.

"They are going to kill him," I cried, pointing toward the exit.

"You go out there, and they will kill you and your father," my mother cried hard, pointing toward me.

"But—"

"No buts. I will not lose you again."

"What about Dad?" I said, raising my voice.

My mother's lips quivered; tears came flowing out of her eyes. Her mouth opened, trying to say something, but nothing came out. I walked over to her, gave her a hug, and allowed her to cry on my shoulder. She held me tight and then slowly released her grip and looked at me. She wiped her tears away and managed to say, "I love your father, but you are the most valuable thing. If I let you out that door, your father will never forgive me."

I nodded in agreement, knowing that I had lost the struggle.

"Aderito, I am waiting," the commander yelled. "You have five seconds before your father dies."

I rushed back to the casement. The commander was standing just to the right. My father was on his knees, shaking. He dialed in, looked through the window, and saw a few eyes looking back. Dad shook his head, telling us not to come, and then mouthed, "It's okay." As he did this, the commander lit the match and dropped it toward my father's head. Time seemed to stand still as the match flipped and toppled over. The flames grew longer, and the match appeared to land on my dad's head. Flames spread from his head all the way to his ankles.

The commander backed up and watched my father as the fire blazed over his saddened eyes.

He screamed. His hands planted on the ground, and he looked up at the casement. I clearly saw his face through the flames. He winced but held on strong for a while; then flames suddenly covered his face, and now I couldn't see any part of his body.

He kept screaming as the flames cut through his flesh and headed down toward his bones. He fell to the ground and rolled several times, took one last scream—and then silence. The body lay on the ground, continuing to burn the flesh, bones, and clothes. He, however, died a while ago.

Soldiers continued to fuel the flames with more firewood, intent on creating ashes of my father.

My mom covered her eyes and cried into her hands. The reverend walked to her and comforted her with a long hug.

I ran away and into my room. I jumped on my bed, face first, and then covered my eyes with my hand. My chest rapidly rose and fell, and my heart pounded. Tears covered my bare hand. I tried to yell, but when I opened my mouth, gasps of air came out. My lips quivered, and my feet began to kick back and forth on the bed.

I grabbed a pillow and managed to yell, allowing the pillow to muffle my sound. I continued to yell, saturating the pillow in my spit and tears, as I got up from the bed and paced back and forth. My hands placed on the top of my head. I looked up at the ceiling. My Adam's apple moved up and down to the same rhythm as my chest.

I walked over to the wall and punched it hard, nearly breaking my hand. I rested my head on the wall and hit the cement until it started to hurt.

My body went limp, and I fell to my knees. I looked back up at the ceiling and said, "Why . . . why are you doing this to me?"

I tried to speak to God, but I felt that he had left me a long time ago. I breathed sporadically in and out; my stomach was shaking, and one tear after the other came from my eyes.

"Why are you doing this? What do you want from me?" I repeated the phrase multiple times, as more saliva formed and exited my mouth.

I desperately needed a sign, something to give me strength, but nothing happened. Lowering my head to the ground, I touched my forehead to the cement. My buttocks stuck in the air, and my eyes fixated on the pool of water made from my tears.

I stayed like this until the door opened. My mother, in tears, walked over to where I lay. I didn't notice her at first. She dropped to her knees and placed her hand on my upper back. I looked up at her. My eyes turned red, and breathing increased to the point that I was hyperventilating. My mother was crying just as hard.

"I am so sorry," she said.

I embraced her as I cried in her arms. I lowered my head to her chest to hear her deep breaths. She continuously rubbed my back. My breathing slowed down, but the tears didn't.

I felt betrayed. God had taken everything. He took Victoria, then the baby, and now he had taken my father. I didn't know what to think, as I didn't have an answer for the life I had led. Confusion clouded the answers as I struggled with my emotions. I was confused if God existed because I couldn't believe that a God that was filled with such love could allow such destruction to exist.

As I lay in my mother's arms, we heard the truck engine start and then drive off down the road. We stayed like this for twenty minutes.

"They have left," the reverend said as he walked into the small room.

I often wondered why the soldiers left without breaking into the house, killing and torturing my mom and the reverend before making their way down the corridor to find me cowering in my room. Perhaps it was God who stopped them, or the commander knew that the brutal torture of my father left me weakened. Moreover, the brittle boy was of no use to the commander. Perhaps he gained satisfaction, knowing that he destroyed my life and I would live in the depths of hell, desperately trying to claw and dig my way out to find some ounce of triumph in my bleak life.

I got up from the floor and walked to the door. I opened it and saw my father's body still burning just under the tree. Neighbors watched him burn from a distance but did nothing. I ran out the door, skidded a few feet in front of the flames, and dropped to my knees.

My eye still reddened, and my clothes soaked with a mixture of sweat and tears. I picked up a handful of dirt and threw it toward the flames.

"Why did you bring us here?" I yelled toward the burning flesh. "Why?" I continued to scream that word, but my voice muted with the sounds of weeping and long gasping breaths.

I had turned my anger from God to my father as I continued to throw dirt in the direction and pound my fists as hard as I could on the ground. My body rocked back and forth, my arms went limp, and I continued to speak under my breath, "Why?"

My mother walked forward. Her hands shook around her mouth. Her knees were shaking. She reached toward my back, and once she was a few inches away, she retracted her hand.

Tired from the crying, pounding, and shaking, I lay on the dirt and continued to look at the flames. I tried to lie with my father once more as I did when I was a child, but I could not embrace him as I was still several feet away from the hot flames.

The flames continued to blaze for the next hour until they slowly died. My mother watched beside me in total shock that the dying flame once engulfed her husband and my father. The flames died down until all that remained was a pile of ashes, a few limbs that were unable to burn, and a blackened head, exposing his skull.

The gale grew heavier, and the ashes were soon blowing in circles around my limp body. At this rate, the ashes would be gone and out of my memory.

I ran into the house. My mother followed, confused at my behavior. I ran to the cupboards and threw the dishes aside until I found a large container with a lid. I rushed back outside, with my mother perplexed but following.

I threw my body near the hot ashes and grabbed a large scoop in my hand, placing them in the container. This continued, one scoop after another, until my body completely covered in the ashes of the fire.

My mother moved toward me and placed her hand on my back and said, "Aderito, what are you doing? Please come inside."

"No," I cried loudly. "He can't go out like this. He needs to have a ceremony."

I continued to pick up his ashes. Trying to go faster than the wind could take them away. I felt as if the breeze were ripping what I had left of my father, without giving me the chance to say good-bye. The container soon filled up, but I continued to pour more into the container, not willing to stop.

My mother grabbed my shoulder, lifted me to my feet, and gave me a hug as the sun was setting in the background. We hugged there for a while. My mother whispered in my ear, "It's okay. We will spread his ashes later."

I grabbed the ashes and walked inside the home, placing the cover over them and walking over to the couch. I sat down and held his ashes on my lap and then squeezed them hard and lay on the couch with my father by my side.

I closed my eyes and wished that he were still there. Hugging his ashes, I tried to get closer to him, but nothing seemed to work. I wished that he never went out there, and that it was my remains that lie in the container, but it wasn't.

While God had taken so much away from me, he had spared my life. I couldn't figure out why my life would be worth so much while my father's not worth enough.

That night I cried myself to sleep, with my father lying next to me and my mother sitting at the kitchen table, watching me grieve, not knowing how she could comfort me. I guess her saying nothing might have been what I needed. I needed the opportunity to grieve and to do this in my own way.

CHAPTER 28

I slept through the evening with the ashes tucked under my arms. When I awoke, I glanced at the cremation and was quickly met with emotions that continued to linger inside from yesterday. My throat became lumpy, my eyes watery, and my stomach churning from side to side as I remembered the burning corpse that turned into ashes that now rested in a small container with little significance.

My mom was sitting at the dinner table, eating breakfast. I got up from the couch, brought the box to the table, saw a plate of eggs and toast waiting for me when I awoke.

"How are you feeling today?"

"Much better. Thanks," I said as I picked up the fork and started to eat.

"I went to the local pay phone and spoke with Grandma last night after you went to bed. She is going to buy the plane tickets for us. They should be ready by tomorrow. She'll confirm the times of our flight later today."

I smiled, and relief came over. The thought of boarding a plane and going back to my homeland was welcomed news. I was a little nervous because I was unsure of how I would fit in or how the other kids would treat me. If people found out what I have done, would they look at me as some criminal that should be sitting on death row or as a troubled kid with a dark past, trying to correct his life?

"We can bring your father's ashes back to the States and spread them in our hometown."

"Mom . . . I was thinking, can we go down to the river and spread them there?"

"Sure, but why there?"

"I don't know. I always felt so at peace down there, and I think that it would be nice for him to be at peace in his home country."

"Then we will go do that today. Eat your breakfast, take a bath, and then we will go."

My mother got up from the table as she finished with her breakfast. I remained for a few more minutes as I scarfed down the remaining food.

The rest of the morning, I took a bath, dressed in my nicest clothes, and waited for my mom to get ready. I had on my only pair of jeans that were purchased a few days ago and a well-pressed buttoned long-sleeved shirt that had about six layers of blue-and-white stripes on top, with the rest of the shirt being a turquoise blue color. I didn't have any black clothes, and I didn't own a suit, so this was the best that I could do.

My mother presented herself from the bedroom. She wore an eloquent black dress that hugged her slender body. The dress went past her knees with a subtle two-inch slit on the sides and thick straps covering most of her upper torso, except for her shoulders. She had on a charming flat pair of black shoes, the only dressy shoes that she owned.

We grabbed the ashes and walked out the door. We strolled side by side to the trailhead and then made the short steep journey to the bottom of the valley. My mother disclosed as we walked down the hill that she had never seen the river because she was too busy with the hospital. I was a little shocked at the confession but understood and was happy that I could see her face light up as she saw the beauty of the place.

She was a little scared to slip down the hill, so she held my arm and walked, trying to time every step so that she didn't trip over some rock and tumble, presenting herself as a fool. I found this to be comical and showed it with my loud laughter as she held my shoulder with a death grip as if the ground would open and she would meet her end. She laughed at herself as she almost tripped over some hard dirt. Seeing her laugh with her mouth widened put a smile on my face and gave me the assurance that it was okay for me to laugh at her expense.

We made our way to the riverbank and stood about three inches from the water. My mother took a deep breath and then placed her arm around my shoulder. She closed her eyes and listened to the wind rustling the trees back and forth and the smell and sounds of the water splashing the bank.

"It is beautiful down here," my mother said.

My mom's eyes moved back and forth; her mouth was wide, and her face gleamed with delight. I was happy to see her looking incredible as the sun lit up her hair and reflected back toward me. I held the ashes in one hand, and with the other, I held the tips of my mom's fingers.

"Do you think Dad is making the trees move like that?"

"I think so."

We stood like this for several minutes. I kicked off my shoes with laces still tied and dug my toes into the dirt. Light splashes of water hit my bare feet, and I was glad to see that my mother had experienced the same sensation as she kicked her shoes to the side.

"Do you want to say anything before we place his ashes in the water?" my mother said in a soft-spoken voice.

"Yes," I gathered my thoughts. "It killed me that I was away from my father for so many years and only got to spend a few days with him before he—" I started to tear up as I was about to say the word. "Died," I managed to utter the word. "Those last few days were special. He saved my life and gave me a reason to live, and I will forever be grateful. I loved him very much, and life will never be the same without him. The time I remembered with him as a child will stay with me forever."

As if Dad were listening to my words, a hard wind blew around my face and whistled in my ear.

I opened the plastic box, took a handful of his ashes out, and threw them in the zephyr. They swirled around, went high into the sky, and then fell to the water. They floated downstream and continued in their path for several more seconds until they could not be seen, and the journey of my father into the afterworld had begun.

"My love . . . my husband of almost sixteen years, we shared some fantastic times and some hard times, but I am so glad that you were a part of my life." My mother wiped away a tear that rolled down her cheek, making her mascara draw black lines vertically down her face. "I will never forget your smile. May you please rest in peace?" she quivered.

My mother followed and grabbed a small handful of ashes and threw them in the gentle breeze to allow nature to carry them into the heavens and down the majestic river.

I handed the lid to my mother. I placed both hands on the box and then dumped the ashes out. Bit by bit, my father's remains poured out of the small rectangular box. Many particles landed in the river straight away while others floated in the air and then sent downstream. The ashes swirled about and stayed on the water's surface for a while. Watching the ashes roll with the river's current and seeing some being taken control of by the wind looked mesmerizing.

As I stood there in a trance, staring at the hypnotic scene, I knew that my father, looking down with his wings spread wide, was creating this magical scene, saying good-bye. The thought brought smiles, tears, and chills up my back; thinking of my father with his arms and wings stretched, waiting to receive one more hug, brought immense satisfaction at that moment.

"Do you know what your father's name means?"

"No," I responded.

"It is a Swahili word that your grandmother heard while she was up north. Your father was born during the times when black people didn't have much freedom in Mozambique and it was ruled by the Portuguese. She heard the name Amani and found out that the name means *peace*. I think that is fitting since you think of this place as so peaceful."

"Can we name this river after Dad?"

"Sure. Should we call it the river of peace?"

"How about Amani's River?"

"I like that." My mother smiled.

My mother held me again in silence as we listened to the wind and watched the last remaining ashes glide downstream, taken by the effortless flow of the river. Neither of us cried because we had done enough of that yesterday. We were both content with standing there, remembering his legacy on this family and prolonging this moment.

Comforted by my mother's embracing arms, I felt the journey that had proven to be so destructive was ending. For the first time that I had been in Mozambique, I felt safe and that no bad person was coming, and I could see the end in sight.

As midday approached and the sun was at its hottest, my mother released me from her arms. I started to walk away, back to the trailhead; but my mother dipped her foot in the water and, with one swift motion, kicked water high into the air, which landed on my back. My shoulders cringed and rose upward toward the tip of my head. My arms went out like a bird's wing, and I turned around and saw my mother with a large grin, laughing as the water soaked into my dress shirt.

I reached my hand in the water and splashed some up into the air toward my mother who tried to escape. We both started to laugh and chase each other in circles. My mother tried to splash me, and then I would retaliate. We continued to do this until we were both drenched.

The laughter and the playful manner of my mother was what I needed. It had been a long time since I played with anyone, and the splendid youthful play was therapeutic on the mind. For too long, I had been too serious and acted more like a barbaric warmonger; and now, perhaps, today was a sign that I could act like a child again, and my juvenile behavior would be cherished and accepted.

I felt guilty that we had such a party atmosphere at my father's funeral, but I knew deep down, he was looking at us with a bright smile and happy to see the two of us laughing and playing the way we used to in the States.

We played like this for a while, and I wished the moment would never stop. I wished that we could run about and jump into the water; but alas, my mother got tired, and we started our journey up the hill.

CHAPTER 29

The house was starting to look empty. Suitcases were sitting by the door, and my mother was rushing through the house cleaning. We gave everything that we couldn't take on the plane to friends in the village. My mother didn't have the money to ship the material back to the States and kept saying that everything is so old that it would be cheaper just to purchase new things or used at garage sales when we arrived home.

I sat on the couch, anxious and waiting for my mother to come back into the room so that we could leave. My legs were getting fidgety, and my eyes moved back and forth. I looked out the window, glancing through the moderately opened curtain, to make sure that no one was waiting. I looked back toward the corridor, waiting for my mother to appear, but all that was heard in the empty house was a faint rustling coming from my mother's room.

A loud pounding came from the door, and the massive knock echoed through the desolate living room. I was just looking out the casement and saw nothing, but now a second knock, louder than the first, pierced through the room.

"Get the door!" my mom shrieked from the back room.

I elevated my body to a standing position and then lumbered toward the front door. The reverend smiled and waited by the doorframe to be invited into the house. I stepped to the side and signaled for him to come in by swiftly moving my hand from left to right with my palm raised to the ceiling. He walked in, taking off his plain black baseball hat. I was a little shocked to see him dressed casually. He usually wore his minister attire; but today, he was wearing a plain blue T-shirt, black cap, and blue jeans.

"Michelle, you ready to go?" he yelled down the corridor.

My mother came from the back room and smiled at the reverend. She then grabbed her purse, which rested on top of the far suitcase, near the couch. We each grabbed a suitcase and exited the house. We made our way to the center of the town. I didn't once look back at the house, and my mother did not care to reminisce about the time we spent there. I think she was ready to leave.

We arrived at the bus that would take us to Maxixe, and then from There, we would catch a bus to Maputo. A small beat-up fourteen-passenger bus was almost full. The bus had windshield that cracked through the middle, which spread out, creating small branches. A small trailer was attached to the back of the van where we placed our luggage.

The reverend shook my hand and then gave me a side hug as he moved toward my mother. He gave her an extended hug and rubbed his hand pleasantly on her back. My mom had whispered in his ear and gave him a kind kiss on his cheek. They let go, and we took our seats in the first bench.

My face was pressed up against the window, looking at the shops, which had just opened. A few more people entered the bus, and finally, we had eighteen crammed in a fourteen-passenger vehicle. The conductor of the vehicle got in and stood up near the sliding door, and the driver followed. The bus started, and we commenced our long journey. We gave one last wave to the reverend, who stood in front of the general store that was a simple kiosk with various items of necessity. He stood there for several minutes, waving to the bus as it journeyed down the road and eventually became a distant memory, gone forever.

Every time we went through a military stop, my insides sank; and I tried to hide myself, not wanting to be seen. When military trucks drove by, I hid my face. When I saw them, I became scared. I didn't want to be captured again, just before we escaped. My mom could sense this because when we saw these men she placed her hand on my knee to offer comfort. I felt like a common criminal, guilty of my murderous past and worried that I would be arrested. There were moments where I felt that I should rot in jail for the war crimes that I committed.

We approached a military stop. It was the FRELIMO troops, stopping the bus. I hoped that I didn't know them. They wore their green frayed military caps low to their eyes. Their green pants were baggy around the waist and ankles. They had heavy shirts that covered their arms, and they dangled their AK-47s toward the ground. They walked around the van and looked at every person. When they approached me, sweat formed on my forehead, and I tried not to shake. A man approached and slowed down as he looked me over, pondering what he should think. He paused slightly. I didn't look at him, so I fixated on a small blotch of dirt that stained the front seat. Desperately, I tried to hide my nervousness, holding my right hand, trying to stop the shaking; but it was near impossible. He must have sensed this. I thought he was going to pull me out, question me, and I didn't think that I would be able to hide it. Would I be taken? Tortured? Or beaten to near death for information? I prayed that he would move on and let the van pass.

I took several deep breaths as he walked past me and waved the driver forward. My time slowed down to a steady beat, and all was normal again.

Once we made our short journey to Maxixe, we transferred to a larger bus that would take us to Maputo. This bus was again packed full of people. We were able to sit near the middle, close to the window. The bus was rather old, and the seats were hard. People carried with them large sacks of goods, chickens, and one man brought on a goat, and I had the unfortunate pleasure of being in front of the smell. I shook my head and even smiled as the man took his seat and held the animal in between his legs. The fellow passengers even laughed, so this must have been unusual to see. The bus gave off a sweaty odor, which forced my head out the bus in search of fresh air. However, the bus parked in the community market where they sold everything from livestock to cookies, so the smell on the outside wasn't much better but was at least not confined.

People in the bus were chatting among themselves, but I couldn't hear anything as I fixated on the horizon. People were trying to sell things, reaching through the windows of the bus. Having it open was an invitation that I wanted to buy. People walked up with baskets on their head filled with bananas, cookies, and various other fruits and vegetables. They sold an eclectic array of products. My mom bought some cookies and a bushel of bananas so that we could eat them on our six-and-half-hour journey into the city.

The bus soon pulled out of the muddy parking lot, leaving the sellers behind as it entered the main road toward Maputo.

I slept for some of the trip, but for most of the journey, I was awake. My eyes looked out the open window and beheld the sights and sounds of Mozambique. I loved watching the passing people walk. Women were carrying large containers of different items on their heads. Their young daughters imitated this act by carrying small containers of water. Young boys played about in the fields while their fathers worked in the gardens, and they stopped to see the passing buses as if it were their entertainment for the day. I enjoyed seeing this because I wished my childhood had turned out this way.

There was a section of the road that overlooked the crystal-blue sound of the Mozambican channel. The sand on the beach was so white it looked like clouds. The water was calm and sparkling, and the people on the beach ran around shirtless in the glistening sun, playing in the water. I couldn't imagine such beauty nestled against such destruction. It was like two different countries and two different worlds so far apart yet so close. This place looked like my sanctuary at the river, so peaceful and calm and the war that ravaged the country so far apart.

On the beach, there were children who had taken four sticks. They placed two sticks about three feet in length in the ground about three feet apart and two more, of equal size, on the other end of the beach about six meters away. The children had taken plastic bags and bunched them tightly, rolled them into a ball, and tied them together and were playing a makeshift game of soccer. They played in their bare feet, shirtless and wearing jeans or shorts that bore distinct holes. The children were carefree, and although I didn't care much for the sport, I wished that I could be there and experience that piece of childhood that I longed to receive.

Alas, the bus passed them, turned inland, and the view of the ocean passed just as quickly as it came to be.

We arrived in Maputo, the capital city of Mozambique. I had forgotten this city and the poverty that lurked at every corner. We pulled into a large muddy parking lot. People were selling goods on both sides of the bus. We got off the bus, and the first thing I noticed was a small child. He had a plastic bottle in his hand and was chewing it intently. He had a buttoned shirt, which had no buttons left. It used to be white but now caked in dirt. His tan shorts had various holes. He didn't have any shoes, his whole body was covered in mud, and flies swarmed around. His face was filled with desperation and poverty. I walked over to the boy and gave him the last banana that I had. His face lit up as I handed it to him like that would be his only meal for the day and perhaps the first that he had in the last few. It struck me how something so small could cause such pleasure. I smiled at the boy and then returned to my mother who was trying to get a taxi to the airport.

We waited for the taxi to pull around, and I noticed many boys and one girl huddled close to each other. They were about my age, and each one had a bottle, which had a brown substance filled to the brim. They were each sniffing their bottles. I was confused at the strange behavior.

"Mom, what are those guys doing?" I asked.

"They have a glue substance in there and are sniffing it to get high, so they don't feel hungry."

I stared at them for the longest time and was amazed that adults passed them and did nothing. I recalled my own experience when adults gave me drugs and alcohol and did nothing, like it was acceptable. This wasn't acceptable. Why don't people care about what others do? I guess they have so many things to worry about; they don't have time to think about other people's kids.

The taxi finally arrived; and we loaded the luggage, got into the car, and drove off to the airport. As we drove through the city, I saw the trash-covered sidewalks. Homeless children were begging for food. More kids on the street sniffing the glue. Desperate faces were at every corner. At one stop light, a man with no legs and no wheelchair pulled himself along the ground. I almost didn't notice him, but I saw a hand thrust up from the ground. It looked like a man's hand, which confused me at first, until I looked down and saw his affliction. He wanted food, money, or anything; but I had nothing to offer.

Right next to the airport, there were many makeshift kiosks. They were thrown together with large sticks, pieces of wood, and metals that they found in people's trash. They looked like they would fall apart at any moment, yet this was where they worked and made a living.

We pulled into the airport, paid the driver, and walked inside the small holding. There was only one place you could sit, and one plane was on the tarmac at any given time. As promised, our tickets were waiting. We provided the details and then stepped into the waiting room with other people heading out of Mozambique. Our plane would take us to Johannesburg, South Africa, and then to New York, and finally back to Texas.

We had waited about an hour before we were directed to head to the plane. We left the small building, entered the hot sun, and walked down the short tarmac. A small plane was directly in front. We walked across the tarmac and up a large flight of stairs and entered to take our seat.

The plane was small and carried about one hundred passengers. There were two columns of seats, and each column had two seats all the way to the back of the plane.

We took our place and waited another thirty to forty minutes before the plane started, and we lifted off the desolate tarmac. As the plane climbed into the sky, I looked down at Maputo. My whole body overcame with relief that I was finally safe. No longer did I have to worry about people lurking over my shoulder. I didn't have to worry about the struggle for democracy that found millions dead and even more affected by the atrocities. I felt that I was a free man and would never have to deal with the ravages of the civil war that ruined my childhood.

PART 5

2013, Spreading Mother's Ashes

CHAPTER 30

Who won? I plastered this question on my notebook when I first arrived back to the States. It was a question that I pondered for decades and was never able to come to an answer. Did the FRELIMO government win because they took control and led Mozambique away from the violence? Perhaps Victoria won! Her life was taken from our planet too early, but her soul was spared from the hell she feared. Was it the Mozambicans who lost their limbs, spirit, and grew to hate while terrorizing people or being terrorized? They are now free, at peace, and maybe they won. On the other hand, maybe it was me, who was able to escape and survive into adulthood.

Looking back at the memories of my life, I have come to an answer: no one. How could anyone win in a savage war? How could a man who lost his arm or the woman her breast come away from such violence and say they have won when they will live with the gnawing memory tugging at their life? How could a young boy who lost his parents or lost his own existence come out of such calamitous acts as being victorious? How could a child who was ripped out of his childhood innocence and reborn into the struggle and forced to kill, rape, and beat honorable people be called a victor? No matter how you look at it, people died, and people were taken by the fiendish hands and turned to mount iniquitous acts. No matter how hard you justified the destruction, people were hurt, and so no one ever won.

My wife sat next to me, with a single tear rolling down her cheek. My son sat in utter shock as I finished the story. I stared at the both of them for a few minutes and waited for them to say something, but they couldn't find the words to describe their feelings. These people had known me most of my life and knew nothing of the shock and horror that I held deep inside for so many years. My wife knew of the war because of the visible marks on my back but knew nothing of the stories. My eyes started to fill with water, and my wife gently rubbed my back and then gave me a warm side hug as my head lowered toward the ground and the harmonious flow of the river was all I could hear. The rushing current that trickled down the rocks and tenuous water rising and splashing against the bank was all I needed to hear. The tears dried up, as I lifted my head to the sky and closed my eyes. I took a swift breath of the smogless air, and a small diminutive smile broke free. I felt at peace in a country that tore me apart.

Coming back here and remembering the story that I left behind so long ago has been bittersweet, and I have sensed many parts of my tragic story on the faces of the citizens who still inhabit the small village. Many live with the visible scars that remind the world of the tragic events, but many live with scars deep within, causing immense pain.

Turning back to the urn, I broke my silence by stating, "That is why we needed to come here to spread my mother's ashes. She wrote in her will that she wanted her ashes spread with her husband. This is the river that I spread my father's ashes in so many years ago."

"It's beautiful," my wife said. My son nodded in agreement.

I grabbed the urn that was still placed next to me and got to my feet. I walked to the river and opened the lid. My wife and son followed, and then we stood side by side, looking at our reflections in the water. I dumped the gray ashes, which floated in the air until they rested in the same spot where my father's ashes spread. There was no breeze like we had so many years ago, but the sight was just as beautiful as the water carried them around and then down the river.

I released one more tear as I said my good-byes to my last parent. I wondered what it might have been like if my mom gave up on me and left back for America. Would I be dead right now? She didn't give up, and she knew that there was a hope that I was alive, and she wasn't prepared to leave the country until she knew of my fate. It was that decision that saved my life.

Looking back at my time as a child in Mozambique, I often have nightmares about it and have seen many therapists over the years. I always come to the same conclusion that I lost my childhood far too young and that war can do nothing but harm citizens who are forced to live with it in their backyards.

I have carried around the scars and the memories of this place. But looking back at the memories, I realized that I can look back and be mad at my father or the RENAMO army; or I can look back and see the strengths, the messages, and tell my story to make a difference in the lives of others. I chose to do the latter, and I am a better man because of it.

I am glad to see that Mozambique is now safe and at peace with newfound successes, and I always looked back at Mozambique, wishing them the best because of the many influential people whom we got to know. For their sake, I have always wished that they were safe, content, and peaceful within their country.

We lost contact with most of the people in the country; but I often reminisce about them and wonder where they are, what they are doing, and if they made it through the darkest period in the history of their country. I always knew or hoped that my premonition was correct and they are free.

I held my wife on one side and my son on the other. We waited several minutes until the ashes of my mother were gone, out of sight, but lingered in our memories. We turned around and started to move up the hill, leaving the river and the country to progress in a flowing majestic pattern. Nevertheless, I will always hold a connection to Mozambique as both of my parents now live down Amani's River.